More Poems from New Zealand

by Hugh Wyles

Hugh Wyles

Original title
More Poems from New Zealand

Cover design
Sonja Smolec

Layout & graphics
Sonja Smolec, Yossi Faybish

Published by
Aquillrelle

Copyright 2011
All rights reserved - © Hugh Wyles

No part of this book may be reproduced or transmitted in any form or by any means, graphic, electronic, or mechanical, including photocopying, recording, taping, or by any information storage retrieval system, without the permission, in writing, from the publisher.

ISBN 978-1-4466-1476-1

Hugh Wyles, an Interview with Jenneddin

At what age did you first start writing poetry?

Round about 8. Boys were writing awful things on lavatory walls and I reckoned I could do better. I did and got caned for it. That was my first masterpiece.

Which poets influenced you and why?

Masefield coz I love the sea. Newbold and Kipling coz I love tales of the British Empire when most of the world was pink and we could kid ourselves it was good. Houseman, Brooke, Owen who preach the futility of war and all other poets, good or bad, because I just love reading poetry.

What draws you to express yourself through poetry?

I enjoy putting my thoughts, dreams, ideas into the English language - especially making it rhyme. I love combining the mental exercise with the inspiration and heartfeel but I often, later, deplore the result.

What type of poetry do you write?

Many types: religious and spiritual, classical and historical, pictorial, sentimental, comical and even satirical and rude. love writing acrostic poems about special AP people whom I have grown to love and admire. I also love writing about beauty in nature and people.

What are the most exciting elements of poetry to you?

The combination of rhythm (metre) and rhyme and the wonderful array of words available in the English language. I also think it's fun to try different forms (as long as they aren't too contrived.)

Do you think of your Muse in personal terms? Are there times when the Muse is most prone to visit?

My Muse is most irregular. Sometimes she will not visit me for days but she always returns with her arms full of ideas. I love her madly.

I'd like to hear about one or some catalyst experiences you've had.

The death of my daughter Vicki was probably the greatest catalyst. We used to write poems to each other when she was alive. I still write poems to her and I wonder if she is somehow working through my Muse?

What are some of the surprising comments you've received?

Oneluckygirl once commented that she actually LIKED one of my poems. I'm probably supposed to have kept this a secret.

What is your step by step for composing a poem?

The first step is to have a subject to write about. The process varies largely from then on, according to the form and style of poem I work at. I would be misleading you to say that I have a workplan for every poem. I mostly work out as it progresses.

What is poetry NOT to you?

It is NOT based on words describing sexual organs or intercourse. It is NOT suicide notes or various recipes for slashing wrists, self-mutilation or drug-induced hallucinations.

It does NOT have to be drenched in self-pitying tears of pain, sorrow and mourning nor need it be achingly lonely.

On the other hand I wish it were NOT a vehicle for sugary effusions of sublime love or the adoration of angels.

Please take a few lines from the best poem you've written (so far) and tell a little about it.

Prayer of Prince Hector of Troy

O' Father of all Gods, this night
I give my life to Thee.
Tomorrow dawns another day.
Its end I may not see.

Please let me die with honour, Lord,
If I indeed must die.
The fate of all my people, Lord,
On my strength will rely.

The movie "TROY" inspired me to write this imaginary prayer of Hector on the eve of his single combat with the Greek Warrior Achilles. Don't know that it's my best so far but it's my most recent pride and I guess hardly anyone will bother to read it.

Is this the end of the interview? Oh! What a pity. I was thoroughly enjoying it. Nice meeting you and thank you.

Table of Contents

More Poems from New Zealand

A Friend Like You	17
A Lost Friend...	18
A Quatern for Jane's Wedding Day	19
Ah! Ne me quitte pas!...	20
Huguelot Castle	21
ANZAC Dawn Parade	21
At the Ball	22
Bastards in Disaster	23
Butterflies	24
Goddess of the Past	24
Culloden	25
Dear God,	26
Do not Forsake Me	27
Earth and Nature	28
Eating in Australia	29
Elfin Snow	31
Faith	32
From an Old Salt	33
How to Make Comments (on Poetry)	35
Hugh Wyles' Favourites	37
Huguelot Mourns for NADIR (MoH)	38
I had a Dream	39
In Response to Margaret's "They Carry Signs"	40
Alfred Edward Housman (1859-1936)	41
Joseph Rudyard Kipling (1865-1936) Part One	43
Joseph Rudyard Kipling (1865-1936) Part Two	47
To Mr. Rudyard Kipling from Hugh Wyles	51
John Kipling (1897-1915)	52
On choosing a Favourite Poet	53
My Son	55
Josephine de Beauharnais (1763-1814)	56
The Black Widow Part One	59
The Black Widow Part Two	61

Testiculados	64
The Seasons of Love	66
I Am the Sea	67
My Favourite Scents	68
My Favourite Sounds	70
Sea Surges	70
Sea Pictures	71
Sea Song	72
Seascape a trilogy	73
The Convict - A Sea Shanty	75
The Mystery of the 'Mari Gaze'	77
The Rime of the Ancient Cucumber	81
The Running Tide	83
The Sands of Time	84
The Tall Ship	84
I Like Women Much Better than Men	85
If…	86
In Case I'm Missed	88
L'abbandonata	89
LostThyme	90
My Epitaph	91
My Garden	92
My love	93
My Problem	94
On Facebook and E-Mail	95
On my Verse Comments	96
Senryu for my sister	96
On Syllables and Meter	97
Pussycat, Pussycat,	99
Remember Us	100
September Snowfall	101
da Vinci's Mona Lisa	102
The Blackbird	102
The Winged Victory	103
Geishas	104
The Epic	105
The Flight of Time	106
The Great Pyramid	107

The Gypsy Life	108
The Little Bench	109
The Lure of The Limerick	110
At the Slave Auction	111
Boobs I'd Love to Feel	113
Cyber Stories	113
"Customer-Service"	114
Join the fight against Terrorism	116
A Word to Islamic Immigrants in Particular	117
On Monogamy	119
Productive Paradise Pairs	120
Roses for you	121
The Sayings of my Nanna	122
The Solution	124
The West Wind	126
War and Peace	126
There was a Time	127
Weather Forecasts	128
Weekend Greetings	129
When the Long Night comes	130
Winter Woes	131
Wintry Weather	132
I loved You	132
Commemoration	133
Tell me, Soldier?	133
December 7. 1941. Pearl Harbour	134
Gas	135
Inhumanity	136
Kiwis and Wars	137
Poppies	138
Reflections in a WWI Cemetery	139
New Zealand Mourns	140
The Bugler	141
The Holocaust Horror	142
The Morning Heroes	144
Dream-Children	145
For a lost daughter, a Lament for Vicki	147
My Beliefs	148

My Blessings 149
More Blessings 151
In Retirement 152
A Sonnet to my Wife 153
A Trio of Tragedies 154
I'll Go with the Gypsies 155
My Best Gift Ever 156
My Commencing 158
My Dislikes 159
My First Love 161
My Love has Left 162
My Muse and I 163
Oh, Let me 163
The Bridegroom 164
The Sexy Secretary 165
The Entered Apprentice 167
The Family Test 168
The Night Before Christmas 170
Walk Naked in New Zealand Day 172
What I Like 173
First Frost 173
A Christmas Gift for a Very Dear Friend 174
A Highland Lassie's Prayer 175
A Maytime Sonnet for a Special Friend 176
A Smoker's Lament 177
Sequel to "A Smoker's Lament" 178
A Timely Lament 179
A Weather Prayer 181
Contemplation 182
Cyber-Love 183
Cyber-Love and Friendship 184
Drought in Canterbury 186
Guests 187
Happy Heart 188
How Are You Today? 188
Happy Mother's Day 189
If Ever 190
If I Am Allowed 192

Mammoth Lovesong	192
Inspiration	193
Irrevocable Time	194
Jack the Ripper	195
Love Poems for the Sick	197
Me and My Muse	198
Message for the Upper Class	200
Midnight Waiter's Blues	202
My Heart is like a Mansion	203
My Last Day	204
Old Age Despair	207
On LOVE and HUGS	208
Sequel to "On LOVE and HUGS"	210
Our Vanishing Friends	211
Past Loves	212
Patience... Impatience	213
Puter Blues	214
Qui pro Patria necavi sunt	215
The Legend of Robin Hood	216
Robin Hood - The Final Shot	217
Sad Loss	220
Swan Song	220
On the Death of a Real Poet	221
Story of a Double-Wash!	222
The Rubaiyat of a Fallen Pear	223
The Self-made Nerd	224
Things to Come	225
To All My (Female) Favourites	226
To My Son, With Love	228
Aussie Boobs	229
More on Boobs	230
More Still on Boobs	233
More Boob Experiences	235
Boobs v. Books	236
In Praise of Ample Femininity	237
Maori Women	238
Rangi and Papa	239
Warring of the Gods	243

Uenuku and the Mist 247
Mataora and Niwareka 252
Rona in the Moon 260
Pania of the Reef 264
The Phantom Canoe 269
The Lost Pink and White Terraces of Rotomahana 272
The Mission Church at Te Mu 273
The Legend of Hinemoa and Tutanekai 274
The Whim of Cleopatra 282

This volume is dedicated with love to my daughter Sue, my wife Edna, and to my supportive friends, in loving memory of my deceased daughters, Victoria (Vickie) and Jacqueline (Jacqui).

More Poems from New Zealand

A Friend Like You

A friend like you can make a dull day bright;
you fill my heart with laughter, love and light.
How oft' a tear you wiped, a smile you made
with rays of sunshine where before was shade,
by simple, loving words you'd speak or write.

My worst predicaments were ever slight
when sympathetic counsel guided right.
No artist or designer yet portrayed
a friend like you.

How often, when I feared to scale the height
of barricades beyond my feeble might,
your helping hand was readily assayed
and I achieved much purpose by your aid.
How, ever in this life, can I requite
a friend like you?

~~~

If, ageing, I should lose my sense or sight,
enveloped in an everlasting night,
with humour sure you'd keep me unafraid;
a friend like you.

dedicated with love to my friends

A Lost Friend...

Once, we were very close we two
Together we sang songs
Together we wrote poetry
We shared our thoughts
We shared ideas
Once, we were very close.

She said I was her guiding light
I'd given her new life
I'd given her vitality
I taught her rhyme
I taught her rhythm
She said I was her light.

She said she was in love with me
I loved her as a friend
I could not love sufficiently
I had a wife
I was not free
She speaks no more to me.

A Quatern for Jane's Wedding Day

Because you are one of my favourite things
as you float down the aisle happily,
I will try not to show how much sadness it brings
that you are not marrying ME.

I will choke back my tears and try hard not to show,
because you are one of my favourite things,
that your wedding to me is a final "No, No!"
and it won't be YOUR call when my telephone rings.

When my whiskers are washed, the fridge purrs, crickets' wings
hum aloud as you trip down the aisle,
because you are one of my favourite things,
though I'm weeping, I'll try hard to smile.

When the joints that are seized only function by half,
my leg aches and that cruel heartburn stings,
I will tell you it only hurts now when I laugh
because you are one of my favourite things.

Ah! Ne me quitte pas!

Ah! Ne me quitte pas! Oh! Please don't leave me.
I'm sorry for those wounding words I said.
I didn't mean them, darling. Please believe me.
Without your love I might as well be dead.

Ah! Ne me quitte pas! Oh! Please don't leave me.
What can I do to show my love is true?
I never really thought that you'd deceive me.
but can't help being jealous over you.

Ah! Ne me quitte pas! Oh! Please don't leave me.
I cannot live if you should go away
For all my foolish words and ways, forgive me.
Come back to me and say that you will stay.

Ah! Ne me quitte pas! I do implore you
I promise I will try to mend my ways
and, if you stay, I'll cherish and adore you
and never doubt you more through all my days.

Huguelot Castle

Amid steep wooded slopes and lofty pines
the Castle *Huguelot* stands, strong and proud.
Its multi-turreted and gothic lines
rise o'er the treetops, noble and unbowed.

Within its walls are centuries of fable
of mediaeval lords and ladies fair.
King Arthur and the knights of his round table
oft-times would visit, sup and sojourn there.
The weary traveller could always find
welcome and warmth inside its lofty halls;
rest for his flagging limbs and peace of mind
as minstrels' music echoed round its walls.

Today it is the haunt of noted poets
who gather to converse and share their rhymes;
a haven, for the few who haply know its
retreat, from all the stress of modern times.

ANZAC Dawn Parade

Not all the words that poets wrote
nor volumes by historians penned,
can animate the dying note
of bugles when the battles end.

And you, my son, who stands before
this cenotaph that bears the name
of men who fought and fell in war;
will you go out and do the same?

At the Ball

You came to me sweetly,
exciting,
so gracefully into my arms.
How could I resist you?
Inviting,
completely enthralled by your charms.

Such moments of rapture,
beseeming,
your head on my shoulder so light.
We moved as if floating,
dreaming.
Ah! Would it had lasted all night!

My arms are now empty,
forsaken.
You've gone with another to dance
and now I must waken,
mistaken,
regretting my forfeited chance.

Bastards in Disaster
or *How Low can they Go?*

In the aftermath of the worst earthquake disaster
in Christchurch City's entire recorded history,
amid many stories of courage and heroism
in the face of danger and irreparable loss,
emerge disgusting tales of extreme baseness
of despicable characters who are taking advantage
of the situation and resulting opportunity
to loot damaged shops and empty houses.

Two sisters who left their shattered apartment
to seek safety in their parents' country home,
returned to find their place completely burgled.
Every cupboard and drawer had been ransacked,
the thieves using a wheelbarrow to ferry
their loot outside to a waiting pickup van
which neighbours viewed without suspicion,
unaware that the girls had gone away.

Two men and a woman were reported;
the woman observed wheeling a fridge
out to the van parked in the driveway.
Neighbours thought that the girls had hired
legitimate removal agents
to salvage their possessions
from the ruined apartment building.
No arrests have so far been made.

Butterflies

I was bringing in the washing from the outside line today
and could not help but watch two monarch butterflies at play.
They swooped, spun, fluttered crazily and chased each other round
above my head or settled for a moment near the ground.

I actually felt quite sad that Nature's such a cad
to let those lovely creatures fly so briefly till they die.
I could not ascertain which was the female of that pair.
For all I know, they might have both been lesbians, or 'queer'.

I hope that they have both derived enjoyment from their flight
for I'm aware that they, alas, will not survive the night.

~~~

*I could not ascertain which was the female of that pair.
For all I know, they might have both been lesbians, or 'queer'.*

Goddess of the Past

Oh Isis! How your beauty haunts my heart
and how your image all my sense enthralls!
Drifting, divine amid these massive halls
Oh Isis! How your beauty haunts my heart.

Egypt's past glory wanes and falls apart.
Pharaoh's great effigy totters now and falls.
Oh Isis! How your beauty haunts my heart
and how your image all my sense enthralls!

Culloden

Tomorrow, when tomorrow comes,
He, who the clansmen led
Wi' skirl o' pipes and beat o' drums,
our Scots blood running red,
may well awa' to save him fly
wi' Florrie to yon Isle o' Skye
or else to fall
or else to fall
as we shall a' be dead the bye.

Tomorrow, when tomorrow comes,
the redcoats will advance
wi' fingers curled and itchy thumbs
round musket, pike and lance.
King Edward issued stern command
direct, to proud Duke Cumberland,
to wipe us out
to wipe us out
and none of us perchance may stand.

Tomorrow, when tomorrow comes,
no crag or croft will shield
a body from those murd'ring scum
yet none of us will yield.
Tho' Edward gain the victory,
no glory his in history
as we who lie
as we who lie
in cold Culloden's misery.

Dear God,

Dear God, now I am seventy-five,
I thank You that I'm still alive.
I thank You for my loving wife
and child who share my love and life;
for love of friends and family
and, most of all, Your Love for me.
For my enjoyments and my ease
and for my many memories,
I thank You. For the pains and grief
from which through You, I seek relief -
I thank You, knowing You will hear
your humble servant's thankful prayer.
I thank You for my upright stature
and my abiding love of Nature;
for all her wonders that I see,
for gifts of sight and sound to me;
for sense of feeling, taste and smell
and understanding thought as well.
I thank You for the firm foundation
provided by my education.
I thank You God, for giving me
my love of prose and poetry
and for a sound and active mind,
to art and music much inclined;
for the technology I need
and all the books that I can read.
I thank You for my home and garden
and, God, I thank You for the pardon
which You so freely grant my way
when thought or action goes astray.
Although it was a bitter pill,
I understand it was Your Will
to take my darling twins away.
Please care for both their souls, I pray.

      Amen.

Do not Forsake Me

Do not forsake me ever, love, I pray.
Without your love my life has nothing more;
I need your hand to guide me on my way.

I thank my God and bless the very day
when, in your eyes, the love-light first I saw.
Do not forsake me ever, love, I pray.

From you apart, I promise not to stray
as I was wont to do in days before.
I need your hand to guide me on my way.

If you should leave my side to go away,
t'would shatter every hope I have in store.
Do not forsake me ever, love, I pray.

Whate'er the future holds we may not say
for God alone will reckon up our score.
I need your hand to guide me on my way.

Inevitable death we cannot stay
yet, when we meet upon that farther shore,
do not forsake me ever, love, I pray;
I need your hand to guide me on my way.

Earth and Nature

Imagine walking in the forest,
tall trees all around,
with dry leaves on the forest floor
and creatures on the ground.

The sunlight filters through the branches;
beams catch tiny flies;
a seedling grows by a fallen tree -
new life where older lies.

Through moss that covers ancient trunk,
where insects eat the wood,
new roots seek moisture from the earth
on which the old tree stood.

The dying growth enriches soil,
feeds plants, insects and worms;
decaying matter turns to food,
sustaining plants in turn.

Earth represents the mother:
stability, security
and universal nurture -
God's nature in its purity.

Eating in Australia

Now I have eaten emu stew
and tasty kangaroo-tail soup.
I've eaten alligator too
but WOMBAT? Yuckk! I would not stoop
to dine on Yemmy's wombat brew.

I've sampled cassowary eggs
and swallowed gallstones of puff adders.
I don't mind kukkaburras' legs
or even platypusses' bladders
but wombat stew is just the dregs.

I'd NEVER eat koala bear
and Yem can keep his stewed wombat.
I couldn't digest all that hair -
In fact, I'd sooner eat my hat
or unwashed lubra's underwear.

Witchetty grubs are fine when fried
and lizards' liver's really tasty
with cactus salad on the side
and dingo dung, rolled in a pastie,
has flavour that is undenied.

Galahs when grilled are fit for kings
and possums' testicles are too.
I love to try those chewy things
like greenback turtle fonderoo
or seasoned flying foxes' wings.

You easily can fill your bellies
with all Australia offers you.
No need for vegemite or jellies
when you light up the barbecue
and you've invited all your rellies.

One thing I always turn down flat
when offerred - that is STEWED WOMBAT!!

Elfin Snow

Goose feathers drifting, drifting down,
Landing with elfin lightness
Like an elfin shroud just sewn.

Swirling, dancing, gently flown,
Soundlessly settling, silent, sightless,
Goose feathers drifting, drifting down.

Slipping from leaden skies windblown,
Layering lawns with lavish whiteness
Like an elfin shroud just sewn.

The snowcapped birdhouse stands alone,
Deserted since mid-winter solstice.
Goose feathers drifting, drifting down.

Covering concrete, colder stone,
Ferns, shrubs and trees with lacy surplice
Like an elfin shroud just sewn.

No strife or struggle, no surprise is shown.
The world lies wrapt in slumbrous stillness.
Goose feathers drifting, drifting down
Like an elfin shroud just sewn.

Faith

Shadows of night surround me
as dark the path I've trod
yet, in the morning, shall I see
my GOD.

Life was ever beautiful;
my faith has made it so
for GOD is with the dutiful
I know.

Now, as my latest hour draws near,
I fear nor death nor grave
for CHRIST, our Saviour Lord, came here
to save.

Though mortal meat blind worms may eat
beneath the heaving sod,
in faith, my soul will rise to meet
my GOD.

From an Old Salt

"Oh I wish's for t' salt sea-air, lad,
'N a sea wind in m' face
'N t' rollin' waves 'n sea-fret,
Well away fr'm this landlocked place.

'N I wish's for t' kick o' t' wheel, lad,
'N t' slappin' o' the sail.
'N the white wake scuddin' aft, lad,
'S I smokes b' t' sternw'd rail.

'R aloft up in t' riggin', lad,
Furlin' them canvas sheets;
'N evr'y bum gits 'is tot 'o rum
As us weighs down in t' streets.

'N t' strainin' o' t' capst'n
'N t' clankin' o' t' chain
'N t' men all singin' cheerful like.
Oh! I wish's I c'd 'ear't again.

'N I wish's for t' creakin' timbers, lad,
O' a movin' ship at sea,
'N t' rollickin' pumps in t' bilge below
'N t' scuppers runnin' free.

'N yer'll never best t' splendour
O' a man-o'-war so fine,
'R t' thrill o' fight 'n t' blindin' light
'S they fire off in t' line.

'R t' roar o' t' heavy guns, lad,
'N t' white-'ot flash o' each
'S they fire in turn n' t' fuses burn
'N they touch 'em to t' breech.

But t' day o' t' sailin's gone, lad,
'N t' tall ships fight no more.
They 'ave either all bin fetched t' port
'R sunk b' some far-off shore.

'N I w'd be back on board, lad,
On a solid timber deck.
'N, when I'm took b' t' Lord, lad,
That's where I w'd go, b' 'eck!"

How to Make Comments (on Poetry)

On no account be honest or sincere
for poets are most sensitive and vain.
Even mildly adverse comment can cause pain
Honest criticism no-one wants to hear.

Remember that the author did his best
give encouragement but NEVER give advice.
To pick on slips or errors isn't nice
nor to get your real reactions off your chest.

To advise or try to help will show your arrogance
and if you should ever try to go too far,
you will just get "Who the hell d'you think you are?"
Remember poets have memories like elephants.

Helpful comments rarely are appreciated,
especially if you try to make suggestions.
Never make replies or answer any questions
unless you want to be reviled and hated.

Use the golden rule in every observation:
"Praise others as you would they should praise you."
Even when you know stern criticism's due,
be diplomatic and avoid all such temptation.

Always give your personal interpretations
even though they may be well wide of the mark.
Make irrelevant remarks, just for a lark.
Try to undermine the author's expectations.

Really lousy comments make no direct reference
to the work itself or any vital section.
The best have absolutely no connection,
dwelling solely on some personal experience.

Copying/pasting entire works from start to end
is a practice lots of commenters employ,
earning tons of extra points they thus enjoy
while sending readers quietly round the bend.

Some examples of the type of words to use
which are proven and have stood the test of time
are "awesome", "great", "amazing" and "sublime".
These are just a few of hundreds you may choose.

If I may, I'd like to sum up in conclusion:
Always read a poem - don't comment before.
The best comment is simply to ignore
but always try to cause complete confusion.

PS: Don't on any account be tempted to applaud.
Costs you seven points that you can ill afford.

Hugh Wyles' Favourites

As friend Del (Nadir) has so correctly stated,
it's impossible to single or select
any special name to be supremely rated
from the list of over forty I respect.

Although the ladies may be stunning beauties,
their poetic talent first drew my attention.
Not, as some think, for routine harem duties
but for lively and original invention.

Of the men whose versatile imagination
I'd be foolish to rate one above the others.
In the feminine and masculine equation
Some are just like sisters, others are my brothers.

Though my favourites may differ in their ends,
I love them all and hope we stay good friends.

Huguelot Mourns for NADIR (MoH)

At Huguelot the silent hall
is hushed, its voices hoarse.
No more the laughter of the Ball
but grief hangs like a heavy pall
for Del, the Master of the Horse,
who ne'er before had suffered fall,
has ridden his last course.

With black the inner walls are hung,
the flag droops at half-mast.
No more the minstrels' songs are sung,
the gates are closed, the bridge is swung.
Sir Nadir, knight, has breathed his last;
a single, tolling bell is rung,
as mourners shuffle past.

The King and Queen are sunk in gloom
the knights and ladies too.
Black crepe is draped in every room,
the castle's frigid as a tomb,
no light comes shining through.
Sir Nadir now has set his plume
upon the unfinished few.

For you, who did not know him well,
t'were good that you should read his work.
Much sound advice his poems spell
and, though his death quite sudden fell,
right to his end he would not shirk
to say whate'er he had to tell.
Sadly we say: "Farewell, dear Del."

on the untimely demise of DEL Warren Livingston, poet and friend.

I had a Dream...

I had a Dream...

I had a dream when I was young
of all the joys of life and living;
of all the songs that could be sung
and all the pleasure I'd be giving

I dreamed of singing on the stage;
I dreamed that I'd become a Diva.
Italian Opera was the rage,
each role enacted with a fever.

I sang on every major stage
with crowds applauding my performance
but, as my voice began to age,
it lost its earlier conformance.

A diva's dreams cannot survive
this cruel, inevitable ageing.
Though she may still remain alive,
when voices die, there ends the staging.

And, where the people used to cheer,
my songs no longer earned applauses
and so I ended my career
with all the former life I'd led...

For, once a singer's voice is gone,
and all her notes sound forced and weary,
it makes no sense to carry on
when everything to sing's been said...

I had a dream to dream when I was young
of all the joys of life and living;
of all the songs that could be sung
but now, I might as well be dead...

In Response to Margaret's "They Carry Signs"

Dear Margaret,

Oh poetess! Thou speakest true,
for many, others' good eschew,
rate their own worth above the rest
and deem their selfish virtue best,
as if the chosen few.

Weekly they occupy their pew
and kneel in sanctimonious prayer
that others may just see them there.
Thou speakest true.

Of that dissembling, canting crew
who slight the work that others do,
few in their never-ending quest
for approbation, pass the test.
They are the opposite of you
who speak so true.

Alfred Edward Housman (1859-1936)

Though born in Worcestershire in England several years before,
his many poignant verses tell of lads who went to war.
Of three and sixty poems which comprise his *"Shropshire Lad"*,
the majority, though beautiful, bespeak a message sad.

His views on life and death were always tinged with pessimism,
yet *"Bredon Hill"* and *"Wenlock Edge"* are steeped in realism.
His style was quite straightforward, free of all obscurity.
"A Shropshire Lad" has been in print since 1893.

While often fatalistic, in his verse until he died,
he never lost his lasting love of English countryside;
particularly Shropshire's little towns and natural beauty
which permeates his poems of human love, life, fate and duty.

His room-mate, Moses Jackson, was the great love of his life
and, after Jackson went away, he never took a wife.
His forty-one unprinted poems, in which he took great pride,
he published as *"Last Poems"* for Jackson just before he died.

His brother, Laurence, published as *"More Poems"*, posthumously,
a further forty-eight and then another twenty-three.
Thus, of all the poems that Housman wrote while he was still alive,
the total in *"Collected Poems"*, is one hundred, seventy-five.

By nature shy, withdrawn, at Cambridge University,
he undertook Professorship of Latin at Trinity.
While there, he wrote (in English) *"Fragments of Greek Tragedy"*
and, in *"Unkind to Unicorns"* some humorous poetry.

Of English verse since Shakespeare, more of Housman saw rebirth
as songs by notable composers like George Butterworth,
Vaughan Williams, Arthur Somervell, young Ivor Gurney too,
John Ireland, Samuel Barber, Wilfred Orr, to name but few.

Remembered as a classicist and scholar of renown,
his grave is at St. Laurence Church in nearby Ludlow Town.

Joseph Rudyard Kipling (1865-1936) Part One

Of the great narrative writer-poets who most appeal to me
I have chosen Rudyard Kipling, not without difficulty.
For Masefield and Macaulay both wrote many a favourite poem,
the one "Songs of the Sea"; the other "Lays of Ancient Rome".

One can't forget that stirring "Elegy" of Thomas Gray
or Omar Khayyam's "Rubaiyat" – unique, each in its way.
Longfellow's "Tales of Hiawatha" cannot be ignored
while, to miss out Tennyson or Walter Scott, I can't afford.

Then, there's Henry Newbolt's rousing stuff like: *"There's a breathless hush..."*
or Banjo Paterson who wrote about Australian bush
or "The Iliad" and "Odyssey" by Homer if you know it,
O, it's virtually impossible to chose one favourite poet...

But I've chosen Kipling first because, through him, I don't forget
the mighty British Empire where "the sun (once) never set"
and, being born before The War, I find his poems inspire
fond memories of childhood years with patriotic fire.

Born in Bombay in India when Victoria was Queen,
while only five with younger sister, Alice, life had been
completely changed when they were both sent, far across the sea,
to England where for six years, he was schooled in misery.

In a lodge in Southsea (Portsmouth) with a couple they would stay,
who took expatriates' children, by the name of Holloway.
In his own autobiography some sixty-five years later
Kipling wrote that *"Mrs. Holloway gave every cause to hate her.*

"From calculated cruelty, combined with sheer neglect,
our only respite for one month each year, we might expect
to visit aunt Georgiana and her husband at "The Grange",
a paradise which, I believe, saved me from growing strange."

In the Spring of 1877 the children's mum returned
from India and, at once from both, their horror story learned.
They were instantly removed and went to live in Westward Ho
where Rudyard, to United Service College, aimed to go.

His aunt would ask him why he'd never told how they were treated
but children, as he said: *"accept as right, whatever's meted
and closely guard the secrets of the prison from a fear
of repercussions otherwise – until they're free and clear."*

His college friendships formed the background to his schoolboy tales
of *Stalky & Co.* (published later) most concerning males.
The school decided that he lacked enough ability
to gain an entrance scholarship to University.

His parents were unable to finance him any more,
so his father then obtained a job for Rudyard in Lahore,
as assistant editor of the *Civil & Military Gazette*
a small but active paper which his future path would set.

And so, he sailed for India in 1882
arriving back in Bombay when the year was nearly through.
It took four days to reach Lahore by slow train from Bombay
and, in that time: *"my English years completely fell away."*

The *Civil & Military Gazette*, for Kipling was to prove,
as he would come to say: *"my Mistress and my most true love"*.
Appearing six days every week throughout the entire year,
although the work was hard, he loved and tackled it with cheer.

His need to write was quite unstoppable, especially when
requested to contribute some short stories from his pen.
He also wrote and published a collection of his verse
as *"Departmental Ditties"* which became his very first.

Each year his one month's annual leave was regularly spent
in the capital of Simla where his family always went.
The Viceroy and the government would spend the summer there
and Kipling came to love the hills and the cooler mountain air.

His thirty-nine short stories which he wrote for the *Gazette*
as *"Plain Tales from the Hills"* were in a prose collection set.
In '88, from the *Gazette*, a transfer made him sad,
from Lahore to the larger *Pioneer* based in Allahabad.

He wrote at a frenetic pace and, in the following year,
as special correspondent for the western *Pioneer*,
he published six collections of short stories he'd begun
which, when completed altogether, totalled forty-one.

He also, for the *Pioneer*, wrote many sketches he
collected later, published in his book :*"From Sea to Sea"*.
In '89, the *Pioneer* relieved him of his duties
but paid him six months salary for notice he disputed.

He sold the rights to many of his stories and decided
to go to London where the literary world abided.
From India he travelled via Rangoon and Singapore,
through Hong Kong, and Japan to San Francisco's golden shore.

From San Francisco, journeying north to Portland, Oregon,
he travelled to Seattle and, from there, to Washington;
then up to Canada, Victoria, Vancouver and B.C.,
then back into the U.S. which he toured extensively.

Through Yellowstone to Salt Lake City; east to Omaha,
Nebraska and Chicago, Ill., then Pennsylvania.
He visited Niagara falls and Washington again,
then Boston and, before he left New York, he met Mark Twain.

He wrote much in his travels and his lectures gained him fame
and his debut in London was received with much acclaim.
His stories were accepted by the leading magazines,
And his apartment in the Strand was well within his means.

His novel called *"The Light that Failed"* was published '91,
"Life's Handicap", short tales of British India, begun
but, most importantly, he met Wolcott Balestier,
a writer from America and formed a friendship there.

The two collaborated on the novel: *"Naulakha",*
named after the pavilion at the Red Fort in Lahore
Kipling suffered nervous breakdown and was told that he should rest,
so he travelled to South Africa which aroused his interest.

He also visited Australia and New Zealand just before
he went to India to see his parents in Lahore.
While there, he learned that Wolcott had, from typhoid fever, died
so he hurried back to England to attend his friend's graveside.

Before return, he telegrammed to Wolcott's sister, Carrie,
expressing his condolence and proposing that they marry.
A telegram reply arrived, much faster than expected,
to thank him for his sympathy and say that she accepted.

They'd met the year before, so knew each other in advance
and, intermittently, had been conducting a romance.
At All Souls Church, in Langham Place, they held their wedding day -
the writer Henry James was there to give the bride away.

dedicated with love to Anissa Gage...

Joseph Rudyard Kipling (1865-1936) Part Two

Carrie and Rudyard Kipling settled on a honeymoon
which took them first to USA where they would visit soon,
the Balestier Vermont Estate, then move on to Japan
but failure of their Nippon Bank enforced a change of plan.

From Yokohama they returned again to USA.
by which time Carrie was already 'in the family way'.
They rented a small cottage on the outskirts of Vermont
"with furnishings of great simplicity, as was our wont."

And, in *Bliss Cottage* on December 29th. was born,
their first child, Josephine, *"my birthday following next morn."*
With snow *"piled to the window-sills, no matter where one looks..."*
came the first dawning of ideas for Kipling's *"Jungle Books".*

With Josephine's arrival, small *Bliss Cottage* felt congested
so the couple, in a plot of rocky hillside land, invested.
Bought from Carrie's brother, Beatty, on this small ten-acre plot,
they built a house named *Naulakha* in honour of Wolcott.

He loved to wander out-of-doors, alone and at his ease,
admiring, in the woods, the turning colours of the trees
or, when there was no snow, down from *Naulakha* he would go
to sit beside the river which meandered far below.

In addition to *"The Jungle Books"* he filled-in countless pages
with poetry and the novel which he named *"Captains Courageous"*.
Some poetry collections in the volume *"Seven Seas"*
were followed by *"Barrack-Room Ballads"* and *"His Apologies"*.

His work was sometimes interrupted. at his most inspired,
by visits from his father who had recently retired
or by other famous writers like his old friend Henry James,
Sir Arthur Conan Doyle and many more with well-known names.

For he, himself, was famous now; his work spread far and wide,
across the USA and UK on the other side.
With Elsie born in '96, you'd think that they would be
most happy and contented as a loving family.

But anti-British sentiment within the USA
and rifts with Carrie's family would drive them soon away.
*"It felt like a decanter which I'd thought was full and stable,
was being aimed at me across a friendly dinner-table".*

They packed all their belongings and they left Vermont for good
and thence set sail for England just as quickly as they could.
They found themselves in Torquay in a house above the sea
where, though he did not like it much, he wrote prolifically.

In August 1897, Carrie birthed a son
on whom his father doted, having named their third child, John.
His *"Just So Stories"* Kipling was already working on,
while *"Kim"*, also for children, instant recognition won.

From '98 the family, for their annual holidays,
would travel to South Africa for quite extended stays.
There, Kipling wrote his poems to support the British cause
for Roberts and all British troops who fought in both Boer Wars.

As "Poet of the Empire", he was always well received
by Cecil Rhodes and Jameson whose doctrines he believed.
He started writing articles, increasingly political,
such as *'The White Man's Burden'* and the poem he called: *"Recessional".*

In 1899 while on a trip to USA,
his daughter, Josephine fell ill and , sadly, passed away.
Although she had pneumonia and no-one was to blame
her parents' subsequent relations never were the same.

In the year of Queen Victoria's death, the Kiplings bought on sight
Batemans in Burwash, Sussex which had no electric light.
*"No bathroom or hot water, built in 1634,
beamed, panelled and original – we could not love it more."*

1907 he won the Nobel Prize for Literature
which, as first English writer, world position did ensure.
His poetry and stories, published widely overseas,
now brought him steady income from substantial royalties.

He published *"Puck of Pook's Hill"* and *"The Fringes of the Fleet"*,
and, at this time, with Henry Rider Haggard, chanced to meet.
The two were "anti-Bolshie" and against "Home-Rule" in Eire;
Kipling wrote the poem *"Ulster"* which his friend did much admire.

Concerned with escalating German military might,
especially their navy as a threat to Britain's right,
he published patriotic poems and pamphlets by the score,
prophetically warning of inevitable war.

When war broke out, although his son was only seventeen,
(his father was his mentor during all the years between)
when Kipling sent the lad down to the army to enlist,
because of feeble eyesight, the initial tests John missed.

So Rudyard used his influence to get his son accepted
for training as an officer although previously rejected.
He managed to get John commissioned in the Irish Guards
though neither could foresee what it would lead to afterwards.

For, on John's eighteenth birthday in the clash at Loos in France,
he was killed by mortar shrapnel in the midst of an advance.
His death left Kipling stunned. He wrote, completely mortified,
"If any question why we died/ Tell them, because our fathers lied."

At *Batemans* he kept writing until 1933.
He died in 1936 on 18th January
just two days prior to the death of Emperor-King, George V;
no English author honoured more than Kipling, while alive.

An initiate to Freemasonry in 1884,
he joined the Perseverance Lodge while living in Lahore.
He was loyal to the Fraternity in spite of everything,
as shown in his *"My Mother Lodge"* and *"The Man Born to be King"*.

In Poets' Corner at Westminster Abbey is his shrine.
His wife survived him by three years till 1939.
His daughter Elsie, married to a diplomat, was left
alone of Rudyard's family, so tragically bereft.

Of all his works, the poem "If" and ballad "Mandalay"
remain, with "Kim" and "Jungle Books", most popular today.

dedicated with love to Anissa Gage...

To Mr. Rudyard Kipling from Hugh Wyles

I've read the tragic poem you entitled "My Boy, Jack"
and I know you lost your daughter, Josephine, a short while back.
Although Life may have favoured you with influence and fame,
Fate is always round the corner and she plays a waiting game.

The loss of one's own child, to any parent, is most terrible.
To lose two out of three, whatever cause, is quite unbearable.
I have myself, lost both my twins – just nineteen years apart
and I well know the anguish of a grieving father's heart.

But, while your Josephine and both my twins were quite unwell,
your son died in an instant from a German mortar shell,
So, though grief-stricken, you can hold your head erect with pride
and know that, doing duty for his Country's sake, he died.

My twins are laid together now, to moulder in their grave
but of John, they found no body parts to bury, send or save.

John Kipling (1897-1915)

John Kipling was the famous author Rudyard's only son
who suffered from short-sightedness since birth and age of one.
At school, he worked assiduously to learn all he was taught,
encouraged by his father though he always failed at sport.

At seventeen when war broke out he tried hard to enlist
and, due to his poor eyesight, entrance tests three times he missed
but Rudyard, through his friendship with Lord Roberts, pressured hard
and got him a commission as Lieutenant, Irish Guard.

John's final letter to his Dad, September, Year '15
tells how, to gain some front-line action, he was really keen
then, only two days later he is given his first chance
to lead his section forward as a part of the advance.

Imagine, stumbling blindly through the mud and driving rain;
he takes his glasses off – can't see, so puts them on again
then, suddenly, amidst the smoke and tumult of all hell,
his light and life's extinguished by exploding mortar shell.

He's blown to bits immediately with all his men around,
no trace of any bodies or remains are ever found.
His waiting father, home at Batemans, writes while reminiscing:
"At last official notice comes to say our son is 'missing'. "

For four more years his parents live in mutual hope and dread,
refusing to believe their son, Lieutenant John, is dead
till finally, when no research brings news of *"My Boy, Jack",*
they're forced to realise that he is never coming back.

Thereafter, Rudyard wrote, with feelings mixed, of guilt and pride:
"If any question why we died, tell them, Because our fathers lied."

dedicated with love to Trish Curtis...

On choosing a Favourite Poet

Purrsanthema, to write about one's 'favourite poet', asks
and thereby sets, for anyone, most difficult of tasks.
Of all the poets great and good who've left their legacy
to single one above the rest's impossible for me.

At school, the works of all the major poets we were taught,
encompassing a wealth of great philosophy and thought.
The beauty of our language was instilled into my mind
and a love of all the poetry great writers left behind.

The obvious choice is Shakespeare whose iambic, metered rhyme
developed English Sonnet form to stand the test of time.
Yet, though I love the Sonnet form, my favourite poetry
is narrative in nature with a base in history.

Of the great narrative writer-poets who most appeal to me
I have chosen Rudyard Kipling, not without difficulty.
For Masefield and Macaulay both wrote many a favourite poem,
the one "Songs of the Sea"; the other "Lays of Ancient Rome".

One can't forget that stirring "Elegy" of Thomas Gray
or Omar Khayyam's "Rubaiyat" – unique, each in its way.
Longfellow's "Tales of Hiawatha" cannot be ignored
while, missing Byron, Keats or Shelley, I could ill afford.

Or Samuel Taylor-Coleridge, who wrote an awful lot
about "The Ancient Mariner" and an Albatross he shot,
and then, Alfred Lord Tennyson and his "Lady of Shalott"
and "The Lay of the Last Minstrel" and other poems of Walter Scott.

There's Henry Newbolt's rousing stuff like: "There's a breathless hush..."
or Banjo Paterson who wrote about Australian bush
or "The Iliad" and "Odyssey" by Homer (if you know it,)
O, it's virtually impossible to choose one favourite poet...

But I've chosen Kipling first because, through him, I don't forget
the days of British Empire where "the sun (once) never set"
and, being born before The War, I find his poems inspire
fond memories of childhood years with patriotic fire.

And there's another reason that I should confess I had:
for Kipling's photos quite remind me of my own Grand-dad .

dedicated with love to Anissa Gage...

My Son

They handed him a uniform, a helmet and a gun
and sent him off to Flanders Fields to swelter in the sun
but, when the fighting started, as it did in heavy rain,
few of thousands who went forward, ever made it back again.

They awarded him a medal called the Military Cross –
a posthumous reward for front-line bravery and loss
but, as he'll never wear it now, I keep it in its box
together with the ribbon and a cutting of his locks.

They have a Roll of Honour where they put his rank and name
but, in a mother's heart, the world will never be the same.
I know he had to go in answer to his country's call
but I wonder why he had to die and sacrifice his all.

and I wonder when these wars and men's hostility will cease
so those who lost and those who live can rest at last in peace.

Josephine de Beauharnais (1763-1814)

Born of previously wealthy Creole whites in Martinique,
from early years possessed of a remarkable physique,
her family had been reduced to dire financial straits
when hurricanes destroyed the sugar crops and their estates.

It happened that her rich paternal aunt, Madame Edmee
was mistress to Francois, the aged Vicomte de Beauharnais
and, in his failing health, arranged affiancement between
his first son, Alexandre and her twelve-year niece, Catherine.

Unfortunately Catherine died before she left for France,
so Josephine was sent instead, her aunt's schemes to advance.
She married Alexandre in December '79
and bore a son and daughter to ensure his family line.

In March of 1794 her husband was arrested;
as aristocratic 'suspects' both, in Carmes jail. were invested.
De Beauharnais was guillotined but Josephine was freed
as the 'Reign of Terror' ended, for her death no further need.

New laws permitted Alexandre's widow to recover
his previous possessions and she soon took up a lover,
becoming mistress of Barras, a leading politician
who introduced Napoleon, relieving his position.

She was a reckless spendthrift who, regardless of expense,
would lavish on her son, Eugene and the younger girl, Hortense
the most extravagant of gifts while her casino bets
accumulated quickly into monumental debts.

The General, though younger, soon became infatuated
with "her elegance and style, low voice, so sweetly modulated".
Described as "having hazel eyes and small, straight nose beneath,
with well-formed mouth kept tightly closed (to hide her faulty teeth),

"of average height, svelte, shapely, of her breasts, a gorgeous pair;
a rather pale complexion crowned with silky, chestnut hair,"
Napoleon proposed to her; in 1796
they married but he'd not consent her creditors to fix.

He left her two days later as he led his 'Grand Armee'
on campaigns lasting several months' in central Italy
and, during separation, Josephine with him afar,
initiated an affair with a handsome young Hussar.

When rumours reached Napoleon, he was infuriated.
His love for her completely changed and never reinstated.
Then, on campaign in Egypt, he began his own affair
with a junior officer's young wife which lasted for a year.

Known as 'Napoleon's Cleopatra', she was never quite
enough to satisfy the General's sexual appetite
and so, with all his fleet destroyed, marooned for several years,
he had affairs with willing wives belonging to his peers.

Though neither blamed the other one for playing the same game,
their marital relationship was never quite the same.
For Josephine considered Bonaparte's affaires were mostly ended
and many of his mistresses she had by now befriended.

He threatened to divorce her as she had not borne his child
but, through the efforts of Hortense, the pair were reconciled.
The daughter pointed out adverse effects from a divorce
on popular opinion, so they let things run their course.

At his crowning as French Emperor in year 1804,
conducted by the Pope with protocol arranged before,
Napoleon placed the crown upon his own head in advance,
and then on Josephine's which made her Empress of all France.

Within a few years it became abundantly quite clear
that Josephine was now unable to produce an heir
and, so he could re-marry and sire children in due course,
reluctantly, she finally agreed to a divorce.

Divorced in 1810, for the remainder of her life,
on good terms with Napoleon who took another wife,
she lived at Chateau Malmaison in outskirts of Paris.
Napoleon, by proxy, wed Duchess Marie-Louise.

A severe bout of pneumonia in May, 1814,
ended the life, at fifty-one, of Empress Josephine.
She was buried in the nearby church of Saint Pierre-Saint Paul,
Hortense interred quite near to her in Malmaison-Rueil.

The Black Widow Part One

Well I, when in Africa, knew a black widow
Her husband, a Zulu, was black as the Ace.
He was killed in the battle of Wongamagdillo
and she, I confess, was the pride of her race.

She was lusty and lithe as a leopard on heat
with lovely long limbs like a lean lioness
and her ebony body, curvaceous and neat,
was surmounted by breasts which I longed to caress.

Now, when widowed there is, for a young Zulu maid,
no future or chance to get married again.
Under strict Zulu law she can't even get laid
so her life is a bore and a bit of a strain.

Of course, for a white man, those laws don't apply
and, purely from pity because of her grief,
I decided, as soon as her boobs caught my eye,
that I, as a Christian, should offer relief.

So I chatted her up in her native Swahili
and I found her most eager with me to cohabit.
Although you may think my behaviour was silly,
with her, I felt much like a randy Jack rabbit.

I would sneak through the kraal every night like a thief
and engage her till dawn when I'd stealthily leave
and, because I provided her constant relief,
she had no cause to suffer or even to grieve.

Now my actual meetings with Zulus were brief
and I did not expect such respect to receive
when the tribe called me 'Bwana' and made me High Chief,
though a few of you may find this hard to believe.

Yet all I have told you is true as I speak.
I'll continue the rest of my story next week.

The Black Widow Part Two

Last week when I left you I said I'd return
to continue the story of the widow who's black
and I know that the outcome you're anxious to learn
so, to honour my promise and tell you, I'm back.

It appears that the Zulus, appraised of my prowess
in providing the widow's much needed relief
from her celibate state in the nocturnal hours,
unexpectedly voted to make me their chief.

Since the time of King Shaka, they'd always admired
perseverance, endurance and strength
and it seems that my feats with the widow inspired
great respect for my vigour and length.

Convinced that I must be their god Nkulumkula,
the warriors banded together to raise
my status as Bwana to that of a ruler,
divine, superhuman, deserving their praise.

As I sat on my throne, they extolled my virility
with singing, carousing, cavorting and dance,
while the maidens queued up, sacrificing virginity
on what they perceived the god had in his pants.

This deflowering of virgins has special significance.
It's known to the Zulus as "Spreading the Ring"
and precedes a young maiden's ensuing concupiscence,
which in turn is denoted as "Ripening in Spring"

Now a man of less vigour would surely succumb
to the onslaught of hundreds of keen Zulu maids,
as each took a turn to present her young bum
to the lap of the god with no conscience of AIDS.

You may think that I found these activities nice,
much multiple, purposeful pleasure acquiring
but, when some of the lustier ones came back twice,
I admit repetition became a bit tiring.

Though most girls were gentle, a few were quite rough
and hurled themselves, recklessly, onto my lap,
yet the strong prophylactics I used for each stuff,
prevented my getting a dose of the clap.

But while I endured this continued exertion,
I failed to consider my widow aside,
who viewed my performance as greedy perversion
and envied each virgin her chance for a ride.

Quite unfortunately, she wrongly presumed
that I was enjoying the feel of each booty.
With mad, jealous rage she became quite consumed
though, as god, I was only performing my duty.

Unmindful of pleasure I'd given her nightly
but wildly inflamed with a vengeful intent,
she seized a loose firebrand, its tip blazing brightly,
and charged at my throne, on destruction hell-bent.

Confronted with danger, I rose up and fled,
pursued by the widow with loud, angry cries
and the whole Zulu impi on foot, which she led,
fully armed with knob kerries and keen assegais.

Well even a god, faced with such a melee,
will summon up strength for withdrawal that's swift.
I ran like a roebuck right down to the sea,
where I leapt in a dory and cast me adrift.

I rowed till my muscles gave out with the strain,
then randomly drifted for days in that dory.
I have never since seen that black widow again
and my next port-of-call was the South coast of Spain
so that is the end of my story.

Now, if you don't believe all this really occurred,
the picture above should provide a much stronger
conviction than my unreliable word,
but remember this happened when I was years younger.

Testiculados

On the South Coast of Spain where I happened to be
pursuing my studies in boobology,
in old Barcelona I ventured one night
to the local corrida to watch a bullfight.

Well, the toreador was a popular hero
who was greeted by loud cries of: "Viva! Torero!"
I admired his cool courage and dexterous skill
as he brought down the bull and stepped in for the kill.

But the slaughter of God's noble creatures I fear
upsets me and causes me soiled underwear.
As I did not enjoy this, I left before long
and went for some dinner to a good restaurant.

From the waiter who served me I asked for advice
as to which local dish he considered most nice.
"Ah Senor, the grilled testiculados is best.
Tonight I can serve if you like to request."

Now I'm always quite partial to anything grilled –
especially meat that I haven't seen killed,
so I nodded assent and said "That will do fine"
and I ordered a flacon of red Spanish wine.

Well, he brought me these two monstrous globes on a plate
which was one of the best meals that I ever ate.
They were succulent, tender, delicious to taste,
and I ate every scrap, leaving nothing to waste.

The following night I went back there again
to savour this great delicacy of Spain
but my waiter said: "Senor, if I may suggest,
the testiculados tonight is not best."

"Allow me to offer our fine sautéed fish
or filet mignon as alternative dish."
I replied: "My good man! On my last night in Spain,
I must have the testiculados again...

"So, from offering anything else, pray desist
Just testiculados pray bring. I insist!"
He shrugged and he gave me a look, as in pain:
"Very well, Senor! Testiculados again!"

As soon as he brought them I straightaway saw
they were nothing at all like the serving before.
These were dry, tough and tasteless, quite wizened and small -
no resemblance to testiculados at all.

I called to the waiter and said: "My good man!
What you have served here tastes like leather-in-tan.
I cannot believe that these things I deplore,
bear any resemblance to the treats of before."

Regretfully speaking while spreading his hands,
he replied: "I do hope the Senor understands."
and then, with a most apologetic grin:
"You see, El Torero does not always win."

The Seasons of Love

In Spring, among the daffodils, my love and I would lie
to hear the high larks singing and observe the clear blue sky.
Beside the cooling waters of the gently flowing stream,
we'd laze the hours away in idle thoughts that lovers dream.

And, through the halcyon summer days, no thought had we nor care
for all the busy people who were working everywhere.
Our families were well-to-do with stately mansions royal;
no need for us to labour or indulge in common toil.

In autumn when the sun was low and lit the golden floor,
the breezes chilled my love till she would lie with me no more.
Her doctors could not diagnose what ailed her more each day
and, as the clouds obscured the sun, she withered slow away.

Then, when the snows of wintertime lay cold and white around,
they took my love away from me and laid her in the ground.
So now, throughout the seasons, I come here to lie alone
and wonder if she's still my love beneath her cold grey stone.

I Am the Sea

I am older than the land.
In the beginning I was the face of the Earth.
I spawned the beginning of Life.
Some left me to breathe the air above
But multitudes thrive within my profundity.
I am home to great leviathans,
Neon worlds swim in my darkest depths;
I am a cold tomb to millions more who challenged me.
Bountiful harvests are cropped from my shoals.
I have borne the vessels of the centuries;
Great ships have crossed my face in majesty –
Many in peace and many in war.
I took them down, dashed them to pieces
Or held them safely – as I willed.

I salt-scent the air and the coasts around me,
I wash the sun-bleached sands of palm-clad tropic shores
Whose beaches run to meet me.
I lash the rocky cliffs of storm-girt islands.
My power is immense, my rages awesome
Yet I can calm with soothing, balmy lullaby,
My hair-fronds swaying gently in my swell.
Ever-changing, unpredictable, untamed.
A pathway for the moon, a mirror for the sun.
The rhythm of my tides ever ebbing and flowing.
I am the Sea – forever free!

My Favourite Scents

Nature's Scents

Of all scents that my garden plots pervade
progressively as seasons come and go,
Lavender and Daphne always steal the show
whether in brilliant sunshine or in shade.

Another favourite scent at any hour
while standing in a field of new-mown hay
as, from damp soil, steam rises and away,
sun breaking through dispels a recent shower.

The breath of salt-scent wafting from the sea
my senses savour and my mind enthrals,
whether in calm or blown by gusting squalls,
just to inhale sea-air is ecstasy.

These are a few of nature's many scents
that never cease my mind to influence.

Man-made Scents

Exotic, fragrant incense slowly burning
is redolent, to me, of former times;
exploring ancient temples, holy shrines
and longing, constantly, to be returning.

A sunny day with friendly folk to gather;
light, happy conversation, drinks and nibbles
as juicy meat, while barbecuing, dribbles.
Ah! That's a scent that I will always savour.

A subtle fragrance, faint, not all-pervading,
just present as she walks into a room;
a woman wearing quality perfume.
Now, that's a scent that heeds no man's persuading.

Whether of Nature or man-made, these scents,
(faint to discern or startlingly intense,)
invoke my memories and stir my sense.

My Favourite Sounds

I love the sound of heavy, drumming rain.
Drumming on a roof of heavy tin.
Its constancy inspires with clear refrain
And draws my watercoloured dreams within.

I love the sound of splashing waterfalls.
Plunging from height to deep and yawning pools.
Cascading over rocky, fern-clad walls
Inspiring thoughts for poets and for fools.

I love the sound of heavy, surging sea.
Surging onto the rocks along the shore.
The rhythm of the soothing surf to me
Calls and enchants my soul forevermore.

These sounds has Mother Nature made for me;
I know no equal man-made melody.

Sea Surges

Surging ocean swells
Ever-rolling waves that lap
Along exotic shores.

Softly, sea-murmurs
Underscore the aching heart,
Restoring courage.
GOD created seas
Even as He made the Earth - and
Saw that it was good.

Sea Pictures

Bare, derelicted sands and tinted skies;
Grey water lapping, cold, along the shore.
Landward the whitecaps race in swift array,
Scudding against the seabirds' mournful cries,
Fling fret-full faces to the wind before,
Like flying horses, tossing manes of spray,
They dive and in the sea-wracked shallows pass away.

Sunlight on the deep green swell and azure blues;
White, lazy clouds on the far horizon lie.
The air is still – a sultry languor creeps
Over a breathless silence and the brilliant hues
Of living coral, far below. On high
A white bird in the sun still flying as he sleeps.
No other sound or movement save the sighing of the deeps.

Rain-slashed, clawing winds and dark storm-clouds;
Wild, angry waters; towering waves that pour
Their fury into wildly swirling gulfs and dive
Onward with flying, threshing foam and fret-clad shrouds
Of ice-cold spray; leaping in manic rage with deafening roar
As though the very elements to rive.
Now lit by lurid lightning... the whole sea is alive!...

Warm night - stars spangled in a warm, exotic sky;
Cool breezes fan the palm-fronds on the shores;
The moon lights a silver pathway on a sea
Of silver waters and the glittering wavelets lie
Rippling, as in a sleep, to a drowsy chorus;
Lulling with slumber-songs, soft music free,
Swelling and ebbing rides in endless tides...
A Tidal Symphony.

Sea Song

Oh! Sing me a song o' the sea, lad,
o' the racing tide and wave
an' the men who sailed an' the men who baled;
the best o' the nation's brave.

Ah! Raleigh, Drake and Hawkins, lad,
were men wot stood right tall.
But best o'the lot, though one arm e'd got,
"Li'l Admiral" high'st of all.

An' sing me a song o' the tall ships, lad,
that were monarchs o' the deep
where the battle runs to the roar of guns
an' them men now lie asleep.

Or sing me a song o' pirates, lad,
o' them swaggerin' buccaneers
an' their treasure-trove in a palm-fringed cove
that I loved in me boyhood years.

Ole Long John Silver an' Pegleg Pete,
Cap'n Morgan an' Deadeye Dick.
'ow they made 'em swank as they walked the plank
or strung 'em up by they're nick.

All those men o' war an' the pirate ships
is gone and will nowt return.
In the deeps they're caught, else safe in port
an' it ain't no use ter yearn.

So sing me a song o' the old times, lad,
all yer steamships youse kin keep.
An' I'll dream o' the ways o' the sailin' days
as I lays me down ter sleep.

Seascape a trilogy

Seascape One... *Island Haven*

Atop the scour-scrubbed timber deck I stand
and gaze across the ocean t'ward the land.
Beyond the rippling waves an island lies
beneath white clouds and sunlit, azure skies.

Soft surf laps languidly along the beach
palm-fringed to where the glist'ning white sands reach.
Around the masthead circling, seabirds fly
white in the sunlight, making mournful cry.

Ah! Would I were a bird to soar the seas
rather than rooted, deckbound, while the breeze
slaps the white sails and sends us scudding fast
to island anchorage; landfall here at last.

A sailor's life is weary, hard and rough
and island paradise is heav'n enough.

Seascape Two... *Seafaring*

Just to escape the smell of pitch and tar,
th' eternal round of rope and hemp and spar,
the endless scrubbing decks, the night-watch stands
or mending sails with raw and frozen hands.

Or, leave the sound of grinding timbers, strained;
the creaking capstan and the anchor chained,
the flapping sail, the crack of windblown sheet,
the whine of icy rigging, rain and sleet:

The howling gales and towering waves that pour
their deluge over decks with deaf'ning roar,
the pitching of the ship in stormy sea
as though all hell's let loose and running free.

These are the trials of a sailing seaman's life.
Scant rest and far from sweetheart, home or wife.

Seascape Three... *Call of the Sea*

Yet, in my mind, fond images I meet:
the awesome sight of ships in line, a fleet
of mighty schooners, anchored side by side,
waiting command to catch the parting tide.

As cargo leaves, new bounty is in place.
Soon paradise will fade yet leave a trace
of evenings spent with native, supped delights
and heady scents, exotic island nights.

Though heaven for some may lie upon the shore
my heart's content when seaward borne once more.
To sail to island shelter such as this
on calm, unruffled sea, is surely bliss.

Ay! There's no other life for such as me.
A seadog never can landlubber be.

The Convict - A Sea Shanty

Alas, my son, what have you done
and where are ye away,
all chained aboard that convict ship
that's bound for Botany Bay?

O' father, I did steal a jewel
that I had better bought.
I took it for my darling girl
who left when I was caught.

Chorus:
Well, thank your lucky stars, me lad,
for mercy in this land.
A convict's life is not so bad
as waiting to be hanged.

The peelers took me to the court,
of jury there was none
Before the judge I straight was brought,
expecting to be hung.

The judge took notice of my tears.
Observing I was young,
he sentenced me to seven years
instead of being hung.

Chorus:
Well, thank your lucky stars, me lad,
for mercy in this land.
A convict's life is not so bad
as waiting to be hanged.

I always wished to travel and
to sail across the sea.
Well now, to far Australia Land
I'll travel there for free.

Say goodbye to my mother please
and tell her not to weep,
There'd be no seven-year release
if I had stole a sheep.

Chorus:
Well, thank yore lucky stars, me lad,
for mercy in this land.
A convict's life is not so bad
as waiting to be hanged.

Goodbye dear father, fare you well,
I'm off to sail the sea,
for seven years of living hell
until they set me free.

I'll never see my girl again
but doubt that she will pine.
She'll soon take up another swain
with better luck than mine.

Chorus:
Well, thank yore lucky stars, me lad,
for mercy in this land.
A convict's life is not so bad
as waiting to be hanged.

The Mystery of the 'Mari Gaze'

There are many tales of bravery
and courage on the sea
but none so bold as them that's told
of Captain Yemassee.

'Twas on the good ship 'Mari Gaze'
from Portland put to sea
and she'd been out for seven days
with a crew of ninety-three.

More stalwart lads you never knew
to ply the Spanish Maine
each member of that valiant crew
had vowed with resolution true
to strike a blow at Spain.

For Britain was at war with Spain
in the days when both were great
and as part of 'New England', Maine
was then an allied State.

And so, it was considered sport
through acts of piracy.
for ships from any Spanish Port
to be sunk or seized at sea.

The 'Mari Gaze' was short but neat
from her sternpost aft and rearward seat
to her figurehead at 'fore.
As darling of the Acadian Fleet
their smallest man o' war.

A sturdy, tidy, trim three-master,
built on classic lines,
when under full sail she was faster
than later-based designs.

Six cannon bore she at each side
at bow and stern two more
her gunners claimed with well-earned pride
to three strikes out of four.

And Yemassee, the Captain bold,
the 'Old Sow' never feared.
His missus was a well-known scold
and so he'd southward swiftly steered
to singe the Spaniard's beard.

The wind blew fair, the wind blew strong,
with billowing sails in motion
the good ship scudded fast along
across the briny ocean.

The lad then from the crow's-nest cried
"Ahoy! A sail! Ahoy!"
and, through his eyeglass, Yem espied
a galleon with great joy.

That Spanish ship of forty guns
is closing on them fast
but Yemassee nor flees nor shuns
but up the Jolly Roger runs
atop his mizzen mast.

The Master's hand upon the helm
is sure as it is steady
to visit Mother Carey's realm
and face death he's quite ready.

He's not afeared o' Davy Jones,
his locker nor his hold.
'Twere better not to make old bones
when married to a scold!

Straight at the mighty galleon he,
ere they can run their guns,
steers underneath that tow'ring lee
and such surprise audacity
the Spanish captain stuns.

"Now, Master-gunner! Light your match
and let your aim not slip!
Pray strike your ball below the hatch
and sink for me this ship!"

The ball flies true and blasts a hole
below the waterline.
Top-heavy, she begins to roll
before the count of nine.

Of near five hundred men at least
who slide into the water
the sharks make quick and ready feast;
to neither Spanish man nor beast
they offer any quarter.

But Yemassee, by pity smote
and feelings of remorse,
bravely he rescues in a boat
six Spaniards and one horse.

As a decent human being Yem
now takes them all on board.
The Spanish Captain, Don Salem,
then offers Yem his sword.

But Yem surveys the six who've braved
the deeps and, as they're males
whom he observes are quite unshaved,
regretting that their lives he'd saved
he lines them 'gainst the rails.

"Now bow yer heads in prayer me lads
and trust ye in The Lord."
Then, just for fun he, one by one,
shoves each one overboard.

Well, truth to tell, he'd had such fun,
he lined up all his crew
and, when they stood there, every one,
he pushed them over too.

Alone, he thought of all the strife
and his unhappy fate
with a nagging, whining, scolding wife
who made such misery of life
being stuck with her as mate.

Overcome with deep depression
and abject misery,
he made his last confession
and he leapt into the sea.

They found the good ship 'Mari Gaze'
adrift in perfect order
and yet, to absolute amaze,
without a soul aboard her!

So now you know the whole story
of the 'Mari Gaze's mystery!

dedicated to the memory of Captain Yemassee

The Rime of the Ancient Cucumber
a sequel to *The Mystery of the 'Mari Gaze'*

As you're aware, the 'Mari Gaze'
had drifted unattended.
Full-rigged, with well-trimmed sails and stays,
she'd made her way for many days -
a mystery never ended.

For those of you who never knew,
perhaps I should explain
how Yemassee and all his crew
entirely disappeared from view
upon the Spanish Maine.

Poor Captain Yem could ill afford
to show his face back home.
for, with abandon untoward,
he'd shoved his whole crew overboard
into the briny foam.

Domestic situation bridal,
mindful of his weal,
he, sore depressed and suicidal,
leaped into the foaming tidal
providing sharks a meal.

Sir Ima Q. (a captain) he,
in his cucumber way,
related this sad history
of nagging wives and misery
upon my Wedding Day.

The wedding guests were not amused
with horror they were smitten
to learn how all his limbs he'd losed
and how he was so badly used
when he by sharks was bitten.

Of course, the rest were all deceased,
no traces left nor marks
for every single man and beast
pushed overboard, became a feast
devoured by hungry sharks.

Those men, once eaten, left no trace;
nor hair, nor teeth, nor bones
and Mother Carey in her place
was left with but an empty space
and so was Davy Jones.

And yet their end was not in vain
although they lost their lives
for they escaped a far worse pain
and nevermore endured again
the threat of nagging wives.

Though Ima Q. had done his best
upon my Wedding Day,
his tale of horror, thus professed,
quite upset every wedding guest
and so they went away.

The story of the 'Mari Gaze'
he did not tell in jest
and afterwards, for several days,
much curiosity would raise
about 'Marie Celeste'.

The Running Tide

The tide is running fast, my lad, and I must fare away.
You've much to do and places still to see
For the trip is long and all too short the day.

The seawind's gusting keen, lad, whipping off the flying spray
And mist is blowing in across the sea.
The tide is running fast, my lad, and I must fare away.

It's a voyage you've to make, my lad, with space for work and play,
And I've no regrets or time for reverie
For the trip is long and all too short the day.

I would fain be by thy side, lad, but alas, I cannot stay
For I hear the sirens' voices calling me.
The tide is running fast, my lad, and I must fare away.

Their call grows more insistent, lad, and I can but obey.
Time is short and this is no eternity
For the trip is long and all too short the day.

I know that when I'm gone, lad, you'll remember me and pray
That I've found safe anchorage where'er I be.
The tide is running fast, my lad, and I must fare away
For the trip is long and all too short the day.

The Sands of Time

time like the tide
rolls on inexorably
with shifting sand

The Tall Ship
An Old Sailor Remembers...

Oh! For the sight of a strong tall ship;
sails filled with a steady wind;
breasting and churning through wave and slip,
leaving long, white wake behind.

And the seagulls circle overhead
beneath the scurrying cloud,
while the man in the foreship swings the lead
as he calls his soundings loud.

And the cannon ranked in even rows
at the gunports open wide,
while the old White Ensign proudly blows
as she breasts the evening tide.

With her decks all battle-ready
and a figurehead at her prow
as her course runs true and steady
while the strong sea-winds allow.

Oh! We fought right many a battle
which we won there on the deep
and, although my old brains rattle,
she's a memory I will keep.

I Like Women Much Better than Men

I like women much better than men
They are truster and more reliable
and I'll say this again and again.

Until they reach two score and ten,
having figures curvaceous and pliable,
I like women much better than men

Over fifty, I think even then
women's beauty is still undeniable
and I'll say this again and again.

Although born of the masculine gen,
with all attributes quite verifiable,
I like women much better than men.

While I get along fine with male ken,
female company's more satisfiable
and I'll say this again and again.

When I'm thinking things out in my den,
my opinion I'm sure's justifiable.
I like women much better than men
and I'll say this again and again

If...

If you can start the day without caffeine,
If you can get along without pep pills,
If you maintain good cheer through each season of the year
and don't bore friends with all your aches and ills,

If you can eat the same food every day
yet never turn it down or be ungrateful,
If you can always say that you'll eat it anyway
and cheerfully demolish every plateful,

If you can understand when all your loved ones
are too preoccupied to pay attention,
or they take it out on you whenever something goes askew
though it's not your fault or cause for their dissension.

If you can take their blame or condemnation
yet never feel resentment or offence,
If you overlook friends' lack of education
and don't correct their want of commonsense,

If you can treat a poor friend or a rich one
with equality of honour and respect,
never trying to disguise with deception, fraud or lies
the truthfulness and frankness they expect,

If you can sleep without the aid of drugs
and don't resort with charlatans or quacks,
If you can conquer tension without medic's intervention
or need alcoholic liquor to relax,

If you can say that, deep within your heart,
you sustain no prejudice or bigotry
against colour, race or creed and you never feel the need
to involve in politics or mutiny,

If you can show goodwill to all your fellows,
If you can love your friends without reserve,
If you always kindly treat any strangers you may meet
and never show alarm or lose your nerve,

If you can do all this, go pick your bone!
You're as good as any dog I've ever known.

In Case I'm Missed...

I want you all to know that my computer's running slow.
My Dial-up server's probably the cause of all my misery
when *Firefox* will not go.

I have to wait an age you see, to get into All-Poetry
to comment on your latest rhyme. I just cannot afford the time
to wait for it to show.

When, finally, I gain entry into the home-page of AP,
I have to wait a further age to transfer to a different page.
Don't know why this is so.

That is the sorry reason why I sometimes let whole days go by
without a visit to AP. Is anybody else like me
and finds the site so slow?

I'm told that Broadband's faster but their terms are a disaster.
With Dial-up I have got a deal that's really very fair I feel.
Broadband costs much more dough.

Perhaps I should not fail to mention that I'm retired and on a pension
so can't afford the fees they set for access to the Internet.
My bank account's quite low.

We certainly can not afford expenses that are untoward
and so, with care I have to tutor how much I spend on my computer
I can't just let things go.

So, if you're waiting there at home, for me to comment on your poem
I hope you'll understand the cause for tardiness of my applause
and not feel undue woe.

L'abbandonata

My lover has abandoned me,
he has no more desire for me!
I throw myself around his knees,
he takes no notice of my pleas.
I weep, I plead, I scream, I faint,
he pays no heed to my complaint.
He tells me to employ restraint.

I throw myself down at his feet,
my eyes he will not deign to meet.
I see his heart has turned to stone,
he goes to leave me on my own.
I tell him I still love him so
as, heedlessly, he turns to go,
My pain he does not want to know.

I feel my heart apart is torn
I would I never had been born.
These flowers I plucked for him before
lie, where he threw them, on the floor.
Like all my hopes and dreams they lie
where, with my love, they start to die.
Oh God! I'm trying not to cry.

If I had known how much I'd pay,
I'd not have let him have his way...

LostThyme

Come, all you tender maidens there,
that flourish in your prime.
Take care to keep your garden fair
that no man steal your thyme.

Once I did have a sprig of thyme,
that flourished night and day
until there came a false young man
who stole my thyme away.

And now, alas, my thyme is gone
and I can plant no new
while that place where my thyme did grow
is over-run with rue.

Now, rue it has deep running roots
that flourish night and day.
I wish that young man would return
who stole my thyme away.

Come back, you false young lover and
don't leave me to complain.
The grass that's trodden underfoot
in time will grow again
but thyme, that's once been broken down,
we hope to heal in vain.

My Epitaph

When my allotted time has run full span
and death has taken those who best knew me,
I leave unfinished much that I began.

Always I tried to be a gentleman
and hope that may preserve my memory
when my allotted time has run full span

I often walked but seldom ever ran.
Though rarely shirking opportunity,
I leave unfinished much that I began.

Whatever I have done or yet still can,
I hope will benefit my family
when my allotted time has run full span.

I hand, to future members of my clan,
these verses though of all my poetry,
I leave unfinished much that I began.

If, on my stone, an epitaph you plan,
forgive me that, through frail mortality,
when my allotted time has run full span,
I leave unfinished much that I began.

My Garden

My garden, of a sudden, seems much brighter;
the flowers more full of colour than before.
Their faces, in the sun, are so much lighter
with happiness and blithesome, gay décor.

An Angel came to stay with us last Friday;
from Sydney Town she fared across the sea.
She came to view my garden, make my day
and also to write poetry with me.

She visited my ducklings with delight
and everything we've shown her brought her pleasure
We've seen the sights together, day and night
and hardly stopped conversing or for leisure.

When angels come to visit from above,
I, and my garden, both respond with love.

My love...

I don't want my love
to change into a bird.
She would fly so high in the sky
my arms could not reach her
my hands could not hold her
and then she would die.
I do not want my love
to become a bird

I don't want my love
to become a princess.
In dress of gold, shoes silver soled
with a crown on her head
but with me in my bed
she would never lie.
I do not want my love
to become a princess.

I don't want my love
to become a queen.
Sat on a throne all alone
but to such a proud seat
I fear my humble feet
could not reach so high
I do not want my love
to become a queen.

My Problem

I have a tricky problem which I don't know how to crack.
My Muse is on vacation and refuses to come back.
For Opera Stories, Histories or Sonnets, without her,
I can't get inspiration so all writing I defer.

To write some worthwhile poetry, I need her by my side
but she will not return till I get rid of Mister Hyde.
She cannot stand the sight of him and says she won't come back
because she thinks he's evil and deserves to get the sack.

I don't know what he's done to her to cause such strong aversion
but I have my suspicions, being aware of his perversion
and if at her, as I suspect, he's tried to make a pass,
he wouldn't stand a Buckley's 'coz he's right out of her class.

But, as you know, it's Mister Hyde who, when I'm feeling stressed,
encourages the stuff I write about the female breast.
For those Booblical Ballads that I write for relaxation,
it's Mister Hyde provides much of my source of inspiration.

Of course, my Muse dues not approve of them or Mister Hyde
and I can't reconcile the two, no matter how I've tried.
So should I now hide Mister Hyde or do I lose my Muse?
If you were faced with this dilemma, which one would you choose?

On Facebook and E-Mail

I recently joined Facebook at request of friend Gregg Rowe.
Anne Barrett warned me that it was an absolute 'time-waster'.
Well, she was right. I doubt if there is any site more slow
so PLEASE use E-MAIL when you message me – it's so much faster.

I find that Facebook, when I click a link, crawls like a snail
to open. Even for the simplest messages, I wait
for up to twenty minutes, whereas stuff sent by E-MAIL
comes through immediately and gives me both the time and date.

Admittedly, on Facebook, one could have a lot of fun
but I just can't afford the time to sit around and wait
for ages when I click the link and loading has begun.
My time to play is rather short and wasting it I hate.

I have a lot of Facebook friends from whom I love to hear,
whose friendships, whether old or new, I value very much.
I love you all and, whether you live far away or near,
I hope you'll use e-mail (and NOT Facebook) to keep in touch.

As a means of instant messaging, Facebook is sheer disaster
so PLEASE use E-MAIL when you message me – it's so much faster.

On my Verse Comments...

I hope folk do appreciate that, when I take the time
to comment on their poetry with some of my own rhyme,
it's not to say mine's any better or that theirs is worse
but to show that what they've written has inspired my flow of verse.

As the singing of a bellbird in my red-leafed maple tree
invites a ready answer from another I can't see,
when reading well-versed poetry which impacts on my mind,
I feel a strong compulsion to respond to it in kind.

I'm sorry if offended folk take umbrage at my ways;
it's simply my intent thereby to show my highest praise.

Senryu for my sister

dark the long night
yet, in the morning
shall she see God.

On Syllables and Meter

Exotic oriental forms
prescribe syllabic count per line
but truly English poetry
requires a metrical design.

Now meter is no wayward thing;
not based on syllables, but **beat**.
Each stress, correctly placed, should sing
with intervening sounds or 'feet'.

Metrical 'feet' comprise each line
providing 'rhythm', 'beat' or 'flow';
just as the bars in classic music
define its measure, fast or slow.

Iambic 'feet' consistently
are one weak followed by a strong.
Anapaests can break monotony
where two weak then a stress belong.

Sonnets and other English forms
mainly employ **Iambic** 'feet',
but there are several other meters
which, in their place, are just as neat.

Dactyllic meter has one strong
syllable followed by two weak.
Two short, preceded by one long
comprise each of a Dactyl's 'feet'.

The Trochee on the other hand
is one strong beat and then one weak.
Trochaic meter is the antithesis
of **Iambic** (both terms Greek!)

Tetrameter has **four** 'feet' per line,
Pentameter's a line of **five**;
Hexameter, with **six** is fine –
Heptameter's **seven** comes alive.

Whichever meter is employed,
the poet must, with care, equate
each stress, ensuring that it falls
naturally, as speech dictates.

Poetry should be read aloud
just as a lyric should be sung.
Silent reading stifles, like a shroud,
the source whence inspiration's sprung.

Pussycat, Pussycat,

Pussycat, pussycat, where have you been?
"To Huguelot Castle to visit The Queen."
And, up at the Castle, what there did you do?
"I sat in the lap of our jolly King Hugh."

When you sat in his lap, were you welcome to stay?
"No. The Queen was quite angry and shooed me away."
Well, that wasn't kindly, why did she do that?
"She can't stand the sight of a dog or a cat.

*"The Queen is afflicted with some sort of allergy
which makes her react with excessive dramaturgy.
Whenever confronted or anywhere near
pussycats, that is something she just cannot bear.*

*"King Hugh, on the other hand, loves dogs and cats
and he, with the Queen, has been known to have spats
but he isn't allowed to let cats through the door
and he always obeys, 'coz he loves the Queen more.*

*"Though the Queen, to prevent it, may constantly try,
the King's never averse to a pet on the sly."*

Remember Us

We are not gone, we do but sleep
in peace at last, all souls as one.
Remember us but do not weep.

As evening shadows softly creep
across graves lit by setting sun,
we are not gone, we do but sleep.

If in your hearts our memories keep
the times we shared in joy and fun,
remember us but do not weep.

Though we no longer laugh or leap
no trip to trek, no race to run,
we are not gone, we do but sleep.

O'er mountain high or ocean deep;
whatever journey you've begun,
remember us but do not weep.

If ought from what we left, you reap
the good that we in life have done,
we are not gone, we do but sleep.
Remember us and do not weep.

Though mortal bodies may not keep
and Time erases every one,
remember us but do not weep.
We are not gone, we do but sleep.

September Snowfall

My world this morn is cloaked in white.
From overhanging, sullen skies
soft, silent snow fell through the night
to greet our waking, with surprise.

Where yesterday were lawns of green,
my world this morn is cloaked in white.
The birds are nowhere to be seen;
they huddle, silent, out of sight.

For children, this is sheer delight;
some never saw the like before.
My world this morn is cloaked in white
and forecasts promise more in store.

The flakes fall fast without abate,
though skies are grey, the light is bright.
Plants bow with unaccustomed weight.
My world this morn is cloaked in white.

da Vinci's Mona Lisa

I don't wish to disparage Leonard da Vinci's taste
but his choice of Mona Lisa, evidently made in haste,
was unfortunate for, if you take away her sickly smile,
the rest of her is hardly the epitome of style.

I suppose he had to make the best of what was then available
though, in Florence, surely girls had charms more prominently saleable.
Most models are notorious for not caring where they sleep
and, maybe, Leonardo liked to do things on the cheap?

Apart from Mona's crowning crop of straggly raven hair,
her cleavage indicates a somewhat mediocre pair.
One cannot help but wonder whether, 'neath that full-length gown,
is concealed a pair of unshaved legs with hair the whole way down.

I don't know what the fuss made of her portrait is about
for I seriously think it calls his judgement into doubt.

The Blackbird

A blackbird sat on my lawn today
to tell me Spring is on it's way
and, though we've all got colds and chills
with all the usual winter ills,
he sang to say that Spring will soon be here
so, in the meantime, be of better cheer.

The Winged Victory

I find it hard to comprehend the Louvre giving space
to damaged sculpture like the Victory of Samothrace
which has no head and, therefore, obviously lacks a face.

I do admit the wings are fine but it's lacking both its arms
and, I confess, it couldn't less display its female charms,
unless one leg exposed incites some narrow-minded ma'ams.

It's stuck atop a flight of stairs in a sort of archway now.
I'm told that it originally graced the ancient prow
of a Rhodean ship two thousand years ago, mounted somehow.

Like lots of other tourists I can't see that it's so great
though, carved from Parian marble, it must be a hefty weight.
Perhaps it sank the ship somewhere within the Rhodean Strait.

To charge poor folk to see bust statues seems, to me, unfair.
I think at least, with superglue, they should attempt repair.

Geishas
from *Travels in Japan*

Once I knew a geisha girl, her name was Cho Cho San.
Her mother was a geisha too. They both lived in Japan.
Whenever I would visit them they'd make a fuss of me
although, as I explained to them: "I just popped in for tea."

As they did not speak English well and my poor Japanese
was not quite good enough to make them understand my pleas,
I failed to prevent them both performing a strip-tease.
The mother first, upon her knees, would take off both my shoes,
while Cho Cho San undid my belt and then removed my trews.

At what was then displayed, they'd clap their hands in geisha glee
and I assume they'd never seen a man as big as me.
Then both of them would touch and stroke and thus increase my size
until what happened next to me should come as no surprise.

I cannot here describe the other things they did to me
for they were very practised in the arts of geishary.
Suffice to say I was completely helpless in their hands,
unable to resist their skilfully applied demands.

They'd say to me: "We like be geisha girls. Have lots of fun
with you Big Boy. You velly big! You be our Numba One!"
I'd thank them both and tell them that their tea was very fine.
(Of Cho Cho's dad I never heard a word or saw a sign.)

Throughout my stay in Yokohama, I can only say
that, being very fond of tea, I went there every day.

dedicated to and was inspired by my suggestive friend Janice M. Pickett

The Epic

An Epic is a lengthy poem
narrating history
which might be real and factual
or just sheer fantasy.
Written in lofty and heroic
style, the form can vary
but is frequently, in Ballad-form,
a running commentary.
It usually celebrates
adventures of some hero
but may extol such villains as
Caligula or Nero.
It also may expound on the
traditions of a nation
or simply be commentary
on current situation.
Whatever is the subject, it is
told with force and strength,
and, though its form is optional,
is noted for its length!
The Iliad and Odyssey
are classical examples;
the Aeneid yet another of
the legendary samples.
I could go on and on and on
but fear your time to waste
so, instead of filling pages, I've
just given you this taste.

The Flight of Time

The bird of Time is on the wing and has already flown;
while sand within the hour-glass runs away
and the clock is ticking faster now than I have ever known...

No time to watch the flowers grow from seeds but lately sown
that we, too tardy, planted yesterday.
The bird of Time is on the wing and has already flown.

When I was man, the world and all it offered was my own
yet all I could achieve was made of clay
and the clock is ticking faster now than I have ever known...

What happened to those years when we in innocence had grown
before we learned to live the adult way?
The bird of Time is on the wing and has already flown.

My ageing body wearies of its aching flesh and bone;
the wrinkled skin and thinning hair now grey
and the clock is ticking faster now than I have ever known...

Soon I must kneel in all humility before God's throne
and, for my trespasses, forgiveness pray.
The bird of Time is on the wing and has already flown
and the clock is ticking faster now than I have ever known...

The friends and kin I loved have gone before yet I alone,
bereft of all companionship here, stay
and the clock is ticking faster now than I have ever known...
The bird of Time is on the wing and has already flown.

The Great Pyramid

I
Khufu
Almighty
with Immutef
architect supreme
did erect in My Name
this enduring monument
to stand for all eternity
as witness to Me the Living God
Ruler of Upper and Lower Egypt.

I
also
had fashioned
for my three wives

A
smaller
one for each
before my own

As
lasting
tribute to
my great favour
towards my consorts.

The Gypsy Life

Oh let me live the Gypsy life
for sure I fain would be
clear of the sordid city's strife
to roam footloose and free.

To tread the open, winding road
wherever it may lead me
and shed myself of every load
from which by choice I freed me.

To park my caravan beside
the highway anywhere
or by the ocean's surging tide
and breathe the open air.

To lay beneath the stars at night
beside my bright campfire
and wonder at the heavens' height,
and inspirations higher.

To glory, far from urban crush,
at mighty God's creation
of mountains, valleys, trees and bush
and my free situation.

To spurn accumulated wealth
or sociable position,
if I have happiness and health
and freedom of condition.

The Little Bench

That little rustic bench of yore
beside the old mill stream,
that's where the two of us would sit
and dream as lovers dream.

That little rustic bench of yore
was made of cedar wood
and there we'd dream the hours away
as often as we could...

That little rustic bench of yore
is broken now in twain,
She would sit there with me no more;
she'd found another swain.

That little rustic bench of yore
has fallen quite apart;
the pieces scattered on the shore
where lies my shattered heart.

O' little rustic bench of yore
become as once you were
and bring her back to me once more;
my love of yesteryear.

The Lure of The Limerick

To write a good limerick is tricky;
the result must be true limericky.
Often based on a rumour,
it's supposed to have humour
and that's where it starts to get sticky.

There are five lines aabba;
the first sets the 'scene' of the play,
while the second exists
to prepare for the twists
which the short third and fourth lines portray.

The concluding line finally acts
as the denouement or climax.
Of same length as the first
it can well be the worst
if in wit or amusement it lacks.

There are few other forms, on inspection,
that can boast of the limerick's perfection.
"Anapaestic" say some,
(ditty DUM, ditty DUM,)
"with iambic dactylic exception".

The form is in essence liturgical,
being derived from Greek tragedy ritual.
Though the meter is mixed,
the rhyme-scheme's always fixed
and the message must always be logical.

At the Slave Auction

Did you have to search far, cruising round in your car,
to locate a secure place to park it?
As I've told you before, there are spaces galore
at the back of the local slave-market.

I went down for a burl 'coz I needed a girl
who could warm up me cold bed at night;
one with whom I could sleep who was going quite cheap
with all female appendages right.

There was one on the stage of a suitable age
with a nice pair of boobs that looked clean
and the shape of her hips made me lick both me lips,
(in between, if you know what I mean.)

Well, they started the bidding and I thought they were kidding.
(I'd have bid up to twenty of course)
but some rich bastard's bid was above fifty quid
which I wouldn't have paid for a horse!

Then I studied her figure and her boobs seemed much bigger
than appeared when I'd looked at them first
and I thought "this sweet honey's worth more of me money"
so I bid all I had in me purse.

Well, we got in me car and we hadn't gone far,
(she was still in a state of undress)
when she undid me fly and proceeded to try
her profound gratitude to express.

She was thankful to me for the size of the fee
I had paid to buy her from the slavers.
She made me understand with her dexterous hand
that she'd make it worthwhile with her favours.

To avoid steering wide, I pulled into the side,
quite distraught from the throb in me knob.
so she shifted her hips and, with vulvular lips,
very quickly completed the job.

I don't mind telling you, that was such a good screw -
quite the best ever had, I confess.
It was clear that I'd gained someone expertly trained
with an outstanding body, no less.

But at auctions like these, there should be a price-freeze
to control all this rising inflation
or the whole slave profession will suffer recession
and their prices will ruin our Nation.

Boobs I'd Love to Feel

Just look at what this beauty shows.
I'd love to get my hands on those
and fondle, with my finger tips,
the firmness of her rising nips.

Her sassy, sexy stance while smoking,
I find incredibly provoking.
In fact, if I get half a chance,
I'd like to get inside her pants

Perhaps she might agree to doff
her dress and take her undies off,
so I could view her, fully nude
and then express my gratitude.

I don't believe I've ever seen
a pair which made me feel so keen.

Cyber Stories...

The words you write are mostly true
for truth's what we expect from you.
Cyber relationships can hide
a seeming angel's other side.
We listen to a tale of woe,
yet never do the true facts know
and certain situations learned,
would make our tears unjustly earned.
Our sympathies may be misplaced
when with true circumstances faced.

"Customer-Service"

The term "Customer-Service" seems, to me, some sort of joke.
I think they only call it that to hoodwink simple folk.
Just try to phone your Bankers or Insurance Company,
or get through to the Airport, the Police or I R D.

If you dial the listed number and, you're lucky to get through,
you get an automated voice which sounds like Doctor Who.
It gives a list of numbers and the options you can use -
if none of them apply to you, you won't know which to choose.

It won't make any difference which number you might press
'coz all their operators suffer twenty-four-hour stress
The voice says they're all busy but "if you'll just hold the line,
somebody will attend to you within the shortest time."

You get some soothing music while you "hold the line" for hours
(their operators may be taking coffee-breaks or showers)
but finally, somebody comes who wakes you with a mutter
in accent you can't understand from Bombay or Calcutta.

I'm sure that more than half the population of New Delhi
or other Indian towns are over here to answer tele-
enquiries and complaints which come in thousands day by day.
They've all been trained to speak that unintelligible way.

Of half-wits, C-S keeps a few (on lowest salaries)
the rest get better jobs with telemarket companies,
so, when you're told "our operators are all busy", you
can bet your bottom dollar that they don't have more than two.

You try to state your problem in a manner cool and sweet
but, every single word or phrase, they ask you to repeat
till, after wasted minutes, you may realise it's wiser
if you insist (before you're pissed) they call their "supervisor".

Eventually, someone who speaks English comes and then,
you carefully explain the reason for your call again.
Well, now you're told: "You must have pressed this number which is wrong -
but to get the right department for you shouldn't take too long..."

They either cut you off or, if they say "I'll put you through",
it seems as though they're re-connecting you to Timbuktu.
Another foreign voice says, as may be anticipated:
"Your voice will be recorded, we are fully automated..."

If you can, just keep your temper cool and treat it all as fun,
but, if it's an emergency, dial 9 or 111.

inspired by the experience of phoning Customer Services at Telstra Clear in Auckland because Pop3 wouldn't authorise me to access my E-mail inbox. I was finally transferred to the Telstra Technical Department (English-speaking Kiwis) who phoned Pop3 and managed to get my problem straightened out

Join the fight against Terrorism

I hope you won't think I am being frivolous or rude
if I ask you for a photo of yourself, completely nude.
For if I have a picture of you in your birthday suit,
I can use it as a weapon to give terrorists the boot.

Once believers see a woman nude who's other than their bride,
Islamic Law compels them to seek death by suicide.
Their place in Paradise with Allah's otherwise denied,
and any share of virgins will be forfeited beside.

The sight of naked females to all Muslims is forbidden
for Allah bids that women even keep their faces hidden.
If I should be subjected to a terrorist attack,
your blown-up picture, held aloft, is sure to drive them back.

As part of our crusade against Islam and all that shit
I know that, as a Christian patriot, you'll do your bit.
One frontal photo for enlargement should be quite enough
and don't delay! Send it today, before things get too tough!.

To: Hugh Wyles in New Zealand in stout envelope please send,
and mark it clearly, on the outside: "AIRMAIL – DO NOT BEND!"

A Word to Islamic Immigrants in Particular

Most New Zealanders are Christians which we ask you to respect.
If you are going to stay here, that's the least we all expect.
Whatever your religion, please abide by Christian rules
and do not be offended that we teach them in our schools.

That English is our language here, you should have known before.
You need to learn it well enough to understand our law.
If able-bodied, get a job which pays you on the whole,
enough to feed your family and keep them off the dole.

With our Kiwi society, we hope you'll integrate
any racial prejudice or violence, we won't tolerate.
We do not want your jihads or your Al Qaeda strife
or Islamic attempt to change our Kiwi way of life.

From the way you treat your womenfolk, we ask you to desist
and, like us, show them courtesy; on this we do insist.
We will not tolerate your stoning women any more.
While here, you are accountable to our New Zealand Law.

If your women wish to show their faces, that is quite OK
If they don't, they will not get a driver's licence anyway.
If you make them dress in black from head to foot, that's your affair
but don't blame us if they, one day, should start to look elsewhere.

Please listen to this sound advice I'm giving you today:
You've come here voluntarily, so live our Kiwi way.
If you think that our way of life's inferior to your own,
you're welcome to repack your bags and take the next flight home.

The same goes for your children who, we hope, are well behaved,
remembering that, from their former lifestyle, they've been saved.
We do not want to see protesting youths with knives or axes
or anti-Kiwi banners while they're living off our taxes.

If you have only come to bludge off our great Welfare State,
and make no effort to contribute or to integrate,
we're sorry that they let you in but let me tell you, mate,
we'll gladly show you through our 'Overseas Departures' gate.

But, if you've come in peace to work, you're welcome here to stay,
We hope you and your family enjoy our Kiwi way.

On Monogamy

Monogamy's unnatural for Man,
restricting to a single mate for life.
Society and Church have placed a ban
on sex with any but one lawful wife
yet instinct drives to get it where one can.

And women must maintain fidelity,
remaining faithful to a single spouse
ensuring thus the strict paternity
of those who will inherit hearth and house
according to routine heredity.

Yet, Presidents and Princes somehow stray
for they are only human like us all
with better chance than most to get their way,
responsive to the power of Nature's call.
and thus along temptation's paths to play.

I sometimes wonder if enlightened races
who practice unashamed polygamy,
in which the wives and husbands change their places
without apparent strife or jealousy,
aren't happier than those who kick the traces.

Productive Paradise Pairs

For those who want to hear about my ducks, I should remark
that, for the last few weeks, I hadn't visited the Park
but, having driven Edna to the Doctor yesterday,
I thought that I might have a look by driving home that way.

My favourite pair were swimming there as I might well expect
and they had not been idle in the weeks of my neglect
for I perceived, to my surprise, that they were not alone
but had a brood of seven fluffy ducklings - quite well grown.

And, further down the river bank, I spied another pair;
the ones called Fred and Maggie who had four new ducklings there.
Because of constant fierce attacks from Darby-drake and Joan,
they'd left the Park and ponds and moved away to be alone.

So, in the intervening weeks, amid the rude earthquakes,
they'd done their duty, conscientiously, as ducks and drakes!

Unfortunately, I must tell you, two did not survive
for yesterday, I have to say, I counted only five.
Stray dogs or cats, eels, water-rats and wicked boys will prey
on ducklings, though their parents try to guard them night and day.

Roses for you...

Behold how bright the roses bloom
Refreshed by morning dew
Such beauty takes but little room
Yet lasts for seasons few.

Those carmine petals soon will pale
When comes the Autumn rain
And, loosing hold, will droop and fail
Nor light my love again.

So let me pluck a bloom or two
While fresh upon their stem
And pass their beauty here to you
Who are as bright as them.

I hope that, by my doing so,
My everlasting love you'll know.

The Sayings of my Nanna

"A bird in hand is worth two in the bushes."
"Make hay while sun is shining – not when raining."
"A sparrow never feasts near where a thrush is."

"The tortoise on the hare is often gaining."
"Two's company but three is sometimes crowded."
"You can't push water uphill without straining."

"Stag's antlers snag which once he would have prouded."
"False flattery, alas, is food for fools."
"One cannot clearly see when face is shrouded."

"It's hard to do good work with worn-out tools."
"Don't stand on ground where miners have been mining."
"Learn first the law before you break the rules."

"Others soon tire of one's incessant whining."
"Pause to say Grace before commencing dining."

~~~

"In ev'ry cloud there is a silver lining."
"While there is life, there's always hope to cling to."
"No storm-clouds gather while the sun is shining."

"If you can sing, first learn a song to sing to."
"A rolling stone will never gather moss."
"A joyful heart, some others, joy can bring to."

"If you lose, try not to moan about your loss."
"A smile will always make the dark clouds scatter."
"If it's hard for servant, harder still for boss."

All these and other sayings she would chatter.
From Aesop many, some from other sources;
there was no limit to her wealth of matter.

"Persuasion's more effective than brute force is."
"You can lead to it but not force drink on horses."

"Only fools will try to kick against the pricks."
"You cannot teach an old dog novel tricks."

The Solution

I've come to an arrangement with my understanding Muse
that she will now return to me and stay,
though I'm slightly conscience-stricken 'coz I feel I've worked a ruse
whereby Mister Hyde is kept out of her way.

It's agreed, for most of every year, my Muse will stay with me.
For Mister Hyde I've found a full-time job
where he will work with women in a clothing factory.
(It's time he earned himself an honest bob!)

The women he'll be working with will suit our Mister Hyde;
broad-minded all, broad-bosomed, factory-fed.
While, for accommodation, he can pay to sleep outside
in Heathcote's reconditioned garden shed.

When Mister Hyde's off work, my Muse will go on holiday
with other Muses who're her chosen buddies
and, during that odd week or so, while she has gone away,
we'll continue with our Boobologic studies.

In the meantime, Mister Hyde has sent the following apology
directed to my Muse in his own hand.
Perhaps our joint on-going collaboration in Boobology,
she'll now condone and better understand.

I hope that this arrangement serves to keep them both apart
but I'm sure Hubertus' letter will have touched my Muse's heart.

~~~

"To Hugh's Muse: June 23rd.2009

*"In recent weeks while you have been away on holiday,
King Hugh has been deprived of inspiration.
Without your help he can't find anything to write or say
but suffers serious cerebral stagnation.
Two female faves, presumably with very good intention,
collected, from the poets on Hugh's list,
a host of Muses at the Castle but I have to mention
that none compared with you and you were missed.*

*"Surrounded by these other Muses, I was forced to note
that, while they are intelligent, it's true,
not one of them would ever, if I had to cast a vote,
for beauty, brains or boobs, compare with you.
I regret my former rudeness which I ask you to forgive.
Please come back to Hugh and earn my thanks as long as I shall live.*

*With apologies, yours most sincerely,
Hubertus Hyde."*

The West Wind

The west wind from the southern skies is blowing
But why it blows there is no human knowing
Rain-clouds above the mountain tops are showing
The westwind from the southern skies is blowing.

Why, heart, is murk and melancholy growing?
My pain and turmoil through my tears is showing.
This wind will set the seeds of sadness sowing
But why it blows there is no human knowing.

The sun has gone, its orb no longer glowing.
With dark of night grief settles, tears are flowing.
The west wind from the southern skies is blowing
But why it blows there is no human knowing.

War and Peace

WAR

Wanton
destructiveness;
ambitious politics
heedless of life or property
wasted.

PEACE

Promotes
conservation,
concern for fellow man,
tolerance, appreciation
and love.

There was a Time

There was a time when I was rash and young,
the days were long and life was worth the living.
My worldly cares had only just begun;
my every wrong, God always was forgiving...
When I was young.

Then, as the years began to pass, I knew
the skies of youth would not remain unclouded.
I lost my wife and, of three daughters, two
and years with pain and misery were shrouded...
As I grew older.

But then I met and wed my second wife
who soothed and wiped away my pain and tears.
With her began anew a happier life
that's lasted now for six and thirty years...
We are in love.

Now weeks speed swiftly by, the days fly fast,
relentless Time allows no rest or pause.
I live each moment as it were my last,
not understanding God's intent or cause...
As I grow old.

Another year tomorrow will be gone
but aches and cares of age will likely stay
and, in the New Year, we will carry on
in hopes of waking to a brighter day...
And thank our God.

Weather Forecasts

The forecast said today'd be fine
around C28
I hung me washing on the line
before it got too late.

They said the morning would be sunny
with a gentle nor-west breeze.
Were they just trying to be funny
or is their aim to tease?

By midday came a howling gale -
it pissed with freezing rain.
Those bloody drongos, without fail,
had got it wrong again.

Me washing all blew off the line
and now it's soiled and wet.
When they say the day will be "quite fine",
how stupid can they get?

And yesterday the bastards said
the day'd be overcast
with heavy storm-clouds overhead
and chilly showers to last.

Well, yesterday was hot and fine
with a sunny, clear blue sky.
If I'd had washing on the line
I would have got it dry.

If yer can't trust them forecasters
and believe their words are true
when they don't foretell disasters,
what the hell's a bloke to do?

Weekend Greetings

A few of you may wonder why so many weeks have passed
since you received the usual "Weekend Greeting" from me last.
Well, as you know, a lot of time's spent caring for my wife,
apart from which, my poetry absorbs much of my life.

In moments left to spare, there's so much music still to hear
and time is unforgiving as I near my eightieth year.
So, what to do, with care I choose in those few hours I'm left to use
and that is why I've discontinued sending weekly news.

As I am now too old for fun and games or youthful capers
and everything you need to know is in the daily papers
or, every night at six o'clock, appears on your TV,
I can't see there is any point in hearing it from me!

There's nothing lately happening in our lives I'd call 'great shakes'
except perhaps, the aftershocks that follow our earthquakes
and, since it seems that recently, they may have reached their peak,
I don't intend to bore you by relating them each week.

I know that, with my greetings, some have said they were impressed
and I hope they find my poetry's of passing interest.
In all my verse I take great care with meter, words and rhyme
and writing it and editing takes up a lot of time.

My friends are not forgotten though and I shall often think
of you and, if you're interested, here's my poetry link:

When the Long Night comes...

When the long night comes, I will not be alone
for, in my sleeping as I recognise,
my family and friends will claim their own.

To heavenly heights by mortal men unknown
as angels bear me up my soul will rise.
When the long night comes, I will not be alone.

All those with whom in life I've loved and grown
will greet me there with pleasure and surprise;
my family and friends will claim their own.

The seeds which I on earth had lately sown
will flower and fruit long after my demise.
When the long night comes, I will not be alone.

Though called upon for misdeeds to atone
if in my faith, correctly I surmise,
my family and friends will claim their own.

For, as I stand before the Almighty's Throne,
and Heaven's Glory first assails my eyes,
when the long night comes, I will not be alone,
my family and friends will claim their own.

Winter Woes

black clouds
murky grey skies
white snow

wind howls
garage roof flaps
door slams

rain cascades
river overflows
drowned gardens

weather forecasters
and crafty politicians
make the worst liars

Wintry Weather

It's a really lousy day today;
the wind is icy, skies are grey;
it seems that winter's here to stay;
the cold and rain won't go away.
At 13C some snow may form;
the Met forecasts a likely storm.
We've set our heat-pump over norm
of twenty-eight, to keep us warm.

I'm sorry, but there's just no way
that I intend in here to stay
and type a greeting out today
when I've got little else to say
except to wish you Happy Day
(and few will read this anyway!)

I loved You...

I loved you once and think I still may do
but cannot say how long my love will last.
Pray, do not let my feelings trouble you
for, in a week or so, they may have passed.

A lovely lass has just moved in next door;
I went across to help her with her chores
and I declare I think I love her more.
She has a bigger pair of boobs than yours.

Your pictures and e-mails were always thrilling
but I have found my neighbour much more willing.

Commemoration

We solemnly commemorate two annual dates:
today, December seven, and the eleventh of September,
when dastardly attacks on the United States
caused monstrous loss of property and lives which we remember.

Deceitful Japanese in nineteen forty one,
with diplomatic peace negotiations under way,
attacked Pearl Harbour. Squadrons dived down from the sun,
and bombed the US battle fleet at anchor in the bay.

With hijacked planes, some Al Qaeda terrorists
destroyed New York's Twin Towers and attacked the Pentagon.
Three thousand died that day according to the lists
and more are dying daily in the fights that carry on.

With heads unbowed we wage war for democracy
and yet we mourn the lives lost in the cause of Liberty.

Tell me, Soldier?

"If you could see that fellow's face, the one you call a "Hun",
Tell me, Soldier, would you fire your gun?

"If you could see his mother's tears as she will mourn that one,
Tell me, Soldier, would you fire your gun?

"If you could see the father's grief, who'll lose his only son,
Tell me, Soldier, would you fire your gun?

"If you could see his children, fatherless before they're bigger,
Tell me, Soldier, will you pull the trigger?"

December 7. 1941. Pearl Harbour

In Hawaii, on a typical sun-drenched, peaceful Sunday morning,
the naval base, Pearl Harbour, was at ease and quite relaxed.
Around Ford Island, heart of the great US. Pacific Fleet,
eight battleships, all lay at rest in neatly anchored rows.
Not far away, the US. army aircraft were assembled,
in ordered groups, at Hickam base or out on Wheeler field.
Everything was quietly shipshape, all the men were spick and span.

From a clear blue sky, incredibly, without the slightest warning,
a wave of Jap Torpedo bombers suddenly attacked.
The damage, within minutes, in the shipyards was complete
with vessel after vessel listing, sinking in death-throes.
Oahu Island, rocked by explosions, literally trembled
as bombers rained destruction down, then for return-run, wheeled
while the fighters mercilessly gunned down men who swam or ran.

~~~

The home airforce, in open fields, was virtually demolished;
planes were bombed or strafed exploding long before they left the ground.
The second Japanese attack which subsequently followed,
though defended, met with practically no air opposition.
The loss of lives and property, beyond all calculation,
was crowned by loss of eighteen very valuable ships.
(By fortune's stroke, all aircraft-carriers chanced to be at sea.)

As a crippling "death-blow", hostile plans were accurate and polished;
their accomplished operation, as surprise, completely sound.
Prior warnings, by incredible bureaucracy, were swallowed
and it left US. in temporary perilous condition.
But treachery served to rouse the anger of a mighty nation
and the Japanese empire, four years later, met apocalypse.
Unconditional surrender followed lost ascendancy.

Gas

In trenches deep with mud and slush each side of no-man's land,
begrimed, unwashed, both weary teams took their accustomed stand.
The temporary cease-fire ended with the break of day
and crosses marked the graves where newly-buried comrades lay.

To end the stalemate using poison gas, the Germans tried
but, fortunately for the Allies, God was on our side.
The wind completely changed direction, blowing wild and wide
back to the German trenches where a hundred thousand died.

They perished in excruciating agony and pain.
Thereafter, 'twas decided not to use such gas again.
But that was WWI; in WWII Nazis would use
a gas called Zyklon B to wipe out sixteen million Jews.

Gas warfare causing painful deaths too horrible to mention,
is totally prohibited by UNO Convention.

Inhumanity

When politicians are inept at finding a solution
to problems that arise between them and some foreign state,
inevitably they will pass a 'solemn' resolution
by force of arms to drive opponents to capitulate.

It may be in the name of GOD or for some other cause;
it's really immaterial what causes their aggression.
Men turn a blind eye to such breach of international laws -
How can either side expect support from godly intercession?

The basic aim of war is your opponent to disarm
while minimizing loss of life to people on your side
and smash into submission those who try to do you harm
irrespective of the deaths of innocents you try to hide.

What sort of men are we who wreak such vengeance cruel and wild
to others in the name of GOD – the more so our own child?

Kiwis and Wars

New Zealand soldiers fought for Britain first against the Boers
and then against Germanic forces in the two World Wars.
With Aussies and Americans they fought the Japanese
and, ever since, they've been involved in fighting overseas.

Our National Anthem is a prayer to God to bring us Peace
but how can He deliver while men's conflicts never cease?
As Christians, we are taught by Christ to love our fellow man,
but what are Allah's teachings in Iraq or in Iran?

How can our children learn the meaning of the Golden Rule,
when all God's Word and Teaching has been banished from their school?
We cannot sensibly expect that God will take our side
when Governments deliberately have His Word denied.

And yet, our future generations well may realise
that wars are not the answer when the world has grown more wise.

Poppies

In Flanders fields red poppies grow.
I've read somewhere that this is so
but poppies scarcely bring us joys
which mark the deaths of countless boys.

I've never viewed a Flanders field
nor seen the poppies it may yield
but know that there, in thousands, died
the flowers of our Nation's pride.

The colour of those poppies: red,
reminds us of the blood they shed
in fighting for our liberty
against the scourge of tyranny.

Their youthful courage failed them not.
Beside their fallen comrades, shot
or shelled or gassed, we know they died
convinced that right was on our side.

So, on Remembrance Day each year,
each one of us should proudly wear
a poppy, just to make it plain
we hope they have not died in vain.

For, sadly, their unselfish cause
was not "The War to End All Wars."

Reflections in a WWI Cemetery

They marched with songs and laughter
to fight their country's war.
Many had never known such close companionship before.

High spirit of adventure
and youth was on their side.
They answered glad the call to arms with righteousness and pride.

They did not know their rival
nor ever saw his face.
Just lads who held opposing space with equal pride of race.

Both sides had firm conviction
that God was with their cause.
"For God and King" one side did sing; "Gott mit uns" sang their foes.

The guns knew neither God nor King
but roared defiant blast
and, miles away good lads each day erupting, screamed their last.

Beneath these serried crosses
fifty-thousand soldiers lie:
companions of those warring sides who marched them out to die.

New Zealand Mourns

White, seried crosses mark each grave of one who died in war,
and signify the life he gave upon some foreign shore.
For all they fought, for all they won, let us remember yet,
Lest we should ever now forget, lest we should now forget.

They fought against the overwhelming might of tyranny
and, by the grace of God, their fight sustained our liberty
So, as the sun shall rise each morn or, in the evening, set,
let us, with each day, not forget, O, let us not forget.

Next year, if we still stand beneath the canopy of Heaven,
this day, we'll pray and quietly say "11/11/11"
and we will stand as we do now and silently our heads we'll bow,
to show that we did not forget, that we did not forget.

Lord God of Hosts Who guards their souls, we pray, be with them yet,
and see that we do not forget, that we do not forget.

The Bugler

I heard the bugler sound his sad lament -
soft breaths at first then swelling to the last.
Forcing the air from lungs to instrument,
from mournful murmur to triumphant blast.

I wondered at it almost mindlessly
how such a basic, automatic action
became a sound that was, so musically,
of mournful yet such rhythmical attraction.

His morning call awakened everyone
then urged them on in their inglorious fight;
taps beckoning them back when day was done
to rest their haggard bodies through the night.

In days to come, his was the voice of hope;
the music by which brave men live and die.
No matter wounds, torn shirts or lack of soap,
'tis courage, not their looks we judge them by.

The fire has died, the bullets spent and yet they charge anew;
lost souls to fight upon this earth, to love, to live, to die.
For what? So their descendants can continue fighting too
the battles they had thought were won for aye.?

The solemn bugler plays his mournful tune.
As bodies, one-by-one are laid to rest,
it lingers over meadow, hill and dune,
fed by the blood of bravest men and best.

The Holocaust Horror

The tale of Nazi calumny
of mankind's inhumanity
is shocking, lasting testament
to millions who through Auschwitz went.
Their piled up shoes bear silent witness
to Nazi views of Jews' unfitness -
the 'cleansing' of this planet's face
of those they thought "inferior race".
Oh! What a mastermind pollution
conceived Hitler's "Final Solution"!
That millions, for their race, should be
gassed to foul death with Zyklon B.
or, if the SS thugs took spite,
clubbed to death or shot on sight
while brainwashed, herzlos, Nazi toffs
strut proudly with their "Totenkopf's".
Auschwitz, Treblinka, Majdanek,
Bergen-Belsen and Belzek,
Dachau, Chelmno, Sobibor,
Mauthausen and dozens more,
Ravensbruck and Sachsenhausen
daily exterminated thousands.
These were the Konzentrationslager
which carried out this sorry saga.
Oh! That such evil came to be
a blot on human history!
Never deny it nor erase
until the end of mankind's days;
for all those millions' ghastly lot
must never be lost or forgot.

They paid, with lives, a price supreme.
Some died with courage, some with scream,
thus we, a lesson stark and stern
should, in remembrance, ever learn:
that evil, though it has its day,
will, in the end, be crushed at bay.
Let all those Neo-Nazi fools
think on th'inevitable rules.

The Morning Heroes

I sing of ancient battle and
Heroic deeds of old
of warrior-bonded mighty band
The fearless and the bold.

No craven wight to flee the fight
No coward to cringe in fear
But strong of arm and stout of heart
Those men of yesteryear.

They were the men who sired our race
And we who, from their seed
Were birthed by British mothers
to meet Britain's hour of need.

We, like our valiant fathers,
stand firm with godly power
that men shall say in later years
"This was their finest hour!"

Dream-Children
after Charles Lamb's *Prose Revery*

One cold night as I dozed in my bachelor's chair
While the flickering firelight flung shadows around
And the sparks from the fir-boughs flew up in the air
Like bright soldiers who march but to die without sound.

I was dreaming of Alice who I'd loved to wed;
Courted her but was spurned after seven long years.
She took up with another as husband instead
Yet I neither condemn her nor smother my tears.

As I half-slept in comfort in my lonely room
Two young children appeared, standing close by my side.
They arose like a mist coming out of the gloom
And surveyed me most mournfully, eyes open wide.

The girl was like Alice. Her blonde hair, her eyes,
Her expression so like it was hard not to feel
That my Alice had come to me. Oh what surprise!
I could not but believe that this vision was real.

And the lad, who at me looked with such solemn gaze
Was, as though in a mirror, myself I perceived.
The resemblance exact could not fail to amaze.
In the dual re-presentment I firmly believed.

"Who then art thou?" I asked them. So melancholy,
Neither spoke but without speech they strangely impressed.
"We are not of your Alice, nor are we of thee.
The children of Alice her husband has blessed."

"We are nought; less than nothing, but dreams - less than air.
We are only what might have been and we must wait
Millions of ages - existence to share
And a name, lost when Alice with you deigned to mate."

I awoke and was quietly alone in my chair.
The fire had burnt low and the room was serene.
Neither vestige nor sign of that heavenly pair -
Just the sadness they left me for what might have been.

For a lost daughter, a Lament for Vicki

When Autumn's fled and all the leaves lie dying
And Winter's icy fingers grip the land,
I'll come to find the place where you are lying
And I will pray and try to understand.

And you will hear, though you are in God's Heaven,
Although your bones lie shallow in your grave,
And you will know your Daddy loves you, even
Though love was not enough your life to save.

I see your pictures hanging on the wall, dear.
My memories are ever fresh and sure,
You'll not grow old, nor age upon you fall there.
In Jesus' arms your spirit will endure.

You went away and now I'll never see you
Until our souls meet in God's Heaven above.
From pain and suffering may the good Lord free you
And never tarnish my enduring love.

My Beliefs...

It's my belief that ALL God's living creatures have a Soul.
A life-force which, at death, returns to God
Who gave it and thereafter He will keep with Him and save.
so Death indeed is not the end of all
but every Soul has life beyond the grave.

The earthly corpse is buried or cremated as may be;
its mortal habitation at an end.
The Soul has left the body at the moment of demise,
its destiny unknown to me or thee.
A mystery unsolved by the most wise.

I can't believe my God is unforgiving - nor selects
only the so-called 'Christian' souls to keep;
Pre-Christians, Buddhists, Islam, all who never heard "The Word"...
shall they be counted valueless rejects?
To cast them all aside would be absurd.

There is much thought that souls return in later life and mould.
Reincarnation is a wide belief.
and spiritualism as a valid faith one should not scorn.
We must permit opinions others hold
and who's to say that none shall be reborn?

Oh God! You give so much but, at our end, You claim the most!
Bereft of Life, all we have owned is dross.
We pray to You, Our Father, to Your Son and Holy Ghost,
yet none will halt or change this final loss
and riches or position will not gain first-past-the-post.

These are my thoughts, the faith on which my firm beliefs are built.
You well may disagree with them but why should blood be spilt?
Not one of us will know, until we reach that farther shore,
what our true fate will be or what, for us, God has in store
and all the world's extremists cannot possibly know more...

My Blessings

I love the world around me and the people I have met
With very few exceptions (who I cheerfully ignore).
I love my God and thank Him for the blessings that I get.
Daily, it seems, from His kind hands, a thousand favours pour.

I've had a most fulfilling life and now am seventy-two.
Inevitably aches and pains and weaknesses befall
But these are merely trifles, which I easily eschew
By counting all my blessings and good fortune overall.

I have travelled many countries and my memories are clear;
I have visited the sepulchres of kings and emperors past;
I have walked in mighty palaces and temples, mausolea
And have learned that wealth and power and even coffins do not last.

I have a loving wife and all our children live good lives
Excepting only one who died in nineteen eighty six.*
I have suffered grief and relished joys but happiness survives
And do not fear my ending notwithstanding Fate's odd tricks.

In faith, I firmly do believe that in the life beyond,
Many souls I love await me and with love my soul will greet.
And I know that God and they with understanding, just and fond,
Will forgive my many weaknesses and past sins when we meet.

But I hope to live for many years, as I would hate to leave
This world I love and all the friends that must be left behind
And I'll leave unwritten poetry for which, alone, I'll grieve,
As I still have much to say and do but Time can be unkind.

On Internet I've met and made some very special friends;
Good folk who, like myself, love writing prose or poetry.
We may not meet in person, for we live at different ends,
But the blessings of the internet allow us colloquy.

This may not be good verse (and I'm afraid it's not my best)
But it does express a few things that I'm trying hard to say
So that when the time shall come for me to take my final rest,
I'll have left a record of my feelings on this blessed day.

sadly, my other twin daughter, Jacqui, died of a cerebral aneurism in February 2005

More Blessings

Among my blessings I must mention two that rule my life:
My love for serious music and for all great English writing.
The former, from an early age, I always found inviting
While the latter was inspired by teachers, reading, and my wife.

My music tastes are catholic but I really thrill to hear
Great symphonies, concertos, tone-poems, operas and such.
While chamber music, solo piano works I love so much
And, of course, the choral repertoire to miss I could not bear.

Ah! Hearing is a blessing for without it I would lose
A tremendous pleasure, failing which, my life would be quite blank.
As I listen every day, my God I most sincerely thank
For the auditory faculty which, constantly, I use.

Sight is another blessing that I would not be without
For the epics and the sagas and the folklore I would miss.
All my library of learning, prose and poetry – all this
I would be so much the poorer not to read – without a doubt.

Worst of all, if Nature's beauties in this World I could not see
And entire inspiration like a desert wasted dry,
If I could no longer see the changing seasons, sea or sky,
My Muse would lose her stimulus to prompt my poetry.

Indeed these are the direst losses I can contemplate
For my reading and my writing and my listening I enjoy
And if these were all denied me how could I my mind employ
In a shroud of dark and deafness? Ah! T'would be a sorry state!

So, for all my many blessings that I, daily, thank My Lord,
Sight and sound are most important - only less than life and health.
I ask not for all the trappings of great power or might or wealth
But for constant capability to write a worthwhile word.

In Retirement...

Please transport me and let me be
on a tropic isle beside the sea
where the breezes play and palm-trees sway
as clouds drift lazily.

and let me lie beneath blue sky
where the single sound is the sea-birds' cry
and the sun-seared sand of a sea-swept strand
is whitened, warmed and dry.

I'll wear no shirt or shoes or socks;
no more you'll see me punching clocks.
for I'm now as free as a man can be -
no need for doors or locks.

I'll leave behind my aches and pains
and give due respite to my brains.
Among my friends I'll apprehend
some losses and some gains.

I'll soon forget the toil and fret
of city life - its stress and sweat;
let cockies keep their cows and sheep
now, free of problems, I shall sleep...
I've cleared my desk and debt.

A Sonnet to my Wife

Chill was the wind, the sky was dismal, grey.
Bleak was the prospect, long the weary way.
I heard your voice – you spoke to me with love
and, once again, the sun shone on my day.

Dark was the night and sleep I sought in vain,
Death was my wish, my soul was filled with pain.
I heard your voice – you spoke to me with love.
My spirit filled with strength; I lived again.

Hard was the trial, the journey lone and drear.
Faint was my heart with misery and fear.
I heard your voice – you spoke to me with love
and life was good because you held me dear.

No obstacle nor wall too high to climb
but words of love lift me to heights sublime..

A Trio of Tragedies
things always happen in threes

It's funny how things always happen in threes.
First, our freezer went bung and the stuff wouldn't freeze.
You could tell by the smell that it wasn't OK
and we threw lots of what had been in it away.

Our heat pump was next then to go on the blink;
the outside compressor is buggered they think.
The technician said it would need some new parts,
so I hope they arrive before next winter starts.

Now the washing machine sounds as though it's gone wrong
'coz an hour for one cycle of washing's too long.
So, tomorrow when Wendy and I change the bed,
it may have to go to the laundry instead,

Eventually, all these three things will get fixed
but there's still the TV or PC to go next
or the toaster or vacuum cleaner to go
and of course all our light bulbs are waiting to blow.

I think that our modern electricity
is just not as good as it once used to be
'coz in those days appliances lasted for years
until now when they suddenly all need repairs.

I'll Go with the Gypsies

I'll go with the gypsies
and, under the stars,
I'll dance to the haunting sounds
of their guitars

And, in the campfire light,
the moon above,
I'll dream in the ecstasy
of nights of love

With wild abandonment,
quite free of care,
I'll follow their caravans,
no matter where

I'll live the gypsy life,
forever free.
The city's ceaseless strife
is not for me.

My Best Gift Ever

My best gift ever was pre-Christmas in 2003
when, quite against my wishes, my wife Edna gave to me
(though I'd said I didn't want one - she replied: "Just wait and see.")
and, in November, turned up with a nearly new PC.

I'd heard that people with computers often got addicted
and spent a lot of time and money on the internet
but I thought I'd play it cool and keep my 'puter hours restricted
for I had a lot of other things to do - please don't forget.

Well this computer, I must say, soon turned my life around.
for many of my interests I discovered as I looked.
A lot of travel sites and other things I quickly found
with GOOGLE-SEARCH and WEBSHOTS.. I became completely hooked.

One night it happened that, when I was surfing randomly,
I chanced upon a link that led me to ALL-POETRY.
Responding to the invitation: "Join up now for FREE",
I signed in, posting my first poem: "A Tidal Symphony".

I'd written verses on and off since I was ten years old
but, I must say, in recent years the urge had grown quite cold.
Reaction to that early poem I posted on AP
encouraged me to try my hand at it more frequently.

Through comments I received and gave, I made a lot of friends.
Though some have staunchly stuck with me I'm rather sad to say
that quite a few have drifted off, pursuing other ends
but I'm thankful for the ones who've come into my life to stay.

Several hundred poems later, I'm most grateful to my wife
for giving, in retirement, a new meaning to my life.
On the one hand I have gained a fount of knowledge that will grow
and it's also brought me many friends who else I would not know.

Yet, equally to this, I owe my deep appreciation
to my parents for the gifts they gave of life and education.

My Commenting

At the start of every morning when I boot up my PC
and click the shortcut icon that leads to All Poetry,
the first page shows each new poem posted by a favourite
which I will then 'bring up' so I can read and savour it.

As you're aware, on any poem entered in contest,
I do not comment, trusting that my doctors know what's best
and they have told me not to spend much longer than one hour
while sitting at my PC or my sight will lose its power.

As well as that my leg goes numb (the blood won't circulate)
and, when it goes into a cramp, that's something that I hate
for, when the pain crawls up until it reaches my behind,
it's difficult to find a worthwhile comment in my mind.

Well, by the time I've read each of the new poems that appear,
my hour has gone and Edna says: "you should come out of there."

My Dislikes

I don't like insincerity and I hate untruths and lies,
I also dislike slimy things and I hate bluebottle flies.
I do not like hypocrisy, deceit or affectation
or snobbery of those who try to act above their station.

I don't mind women's painted toes as long as they are neat
but one thing that will turn me off is dirty, smelly feet.
I do like strappy sandals but thigh-boots I'd never choose
I prefer two shapely ankles in a pair of high-heeled shoes.

I don't like whining women but won't tolerate-abuse
I utterly detest pierced lips or females with tattoos.
I can't abide those filthy folk who pick their snotty noses.
I don't like being scratched by thorns but otherwise love roses

I don't like dirty finger-nails or hairy-chested males
or macho guys whose only talent's telling smutty tales.
I don't like seeing anyone in public scratch their bum
and I get annoyed with people who incessantly chew gum.

I hate those TV adverts where they have loud music braying
that drowns completely anything the advertiser's saying
and I can't stand those presenters who enunciate so fast,
that they're unintelligible from the first word to their last.

I hate it when folk ring me and I rush to grab the phone,
I pick up the receiver, speak, but answer is there none.
That stupid people can't get numbers right is no surprise
but surely decency dictates they should apologise.

I don't like exercises and can never see the sense
in boxing, wrestling, or in other forms of violence..
I utterly abhor abuse of wives or juveniles
and think they ought to hang all murderers and paedophiles.

In fact, they should reintroduce the old death penalty
for any form of murder, rape or drug prolifery.
The perpetrators of such crimes are fiends of little worth;
destroying others, they should forfeit any place on earth.

Those are a few of my dislikes which I have set in rhyme,
I can think of several others when I get a bit more time.

My First Love

At the Palace 'Herrenchiemsee' I first met her
in summertime when she was on her own.
Although 'twas long ago, I'll not forget her -
we strolled around the gardens hand-in-hand and quite alone.

I photographed her seated by the fountains
which represent the mounted goddess Fame.
Together, in the high Bavarian mountains,
we visited King Ludwig's Chateau, 'Linderhof' by name.

'Twas by the marble Venus Temple there
she gave her love to me; I gave her mine.
As a pair we lived together through that year,
exploring 'Hohenschwangau' and the Castle 'Neuschwanstein'.

But happy holidays must have their ends -
so she returned to university.
We vowed that we would always be good friends.
although my kiwi home is distant, far from Germany.

By February's end we were apart
though we conversed a few times when on line.
She'll always have a place within my heart -
for, of all others, she remains my first true Valentine.

She married someone else and that's the last I heard from Ruth
but I can't forget those castles or that summer of our youth.

My Love has Left

Alas! My love has left and gone away -
Away to reach some farther shore unknown.
Unknown, forever closed to light of day,
Daylight that brightens not this soul alone.

Alone, I face the world apart, bereft -
Bereft of her who was my very life.
Life ended on the very day she left -
Left me without my confidant or wife.

Wife she had been to me for thirty years -
Years that were very like a golden age.
Age was forever foremost of our fears -
Fears of the future and the unknown page.

Page me my love through heaven's golden gate!
Gate to the path whereon my love will wait.

My Muse and I

My Muse and I, while words belie,
are actually rather shy
Though inspiration's from above
we thrive on faves' support and love
but, if nobody reads our work,
the AP site we fain might shirk.

We see no profitable use
to write verse which is poor excuse
for leaving work of greater worth
when readers are so down-to-earth,
too busy with their daily need
to spend their time to pause and read.

But, if we don't appear some days,
don't think that poets ever laze.

Oh, Let me...

Oh let me sail away with you and let us ride the deeps,
Oh let me sip your wine and taste your honeyed bread and butter,
Oh let me sup the nectar of those lips I love for keeps
and listen to the music of each soothing word you utter.

Then shall I cross a sea unknown to an undiscovered place
where chilly winds have never blown the softness in my face.
and we shall sail in a faster ship to the rim of a vaster sea
than rapture or companionship were ever dear to me.

The Bridegroom

My love may ne'er again see me
nor will I see her more
for I must go to sea

The Press Gang nabbed me, one, two, three,
as I came through the door.
My love may ne'er again see me.

They dragged me, fighting furiously.
My love stood, screaming sore
nor will I see her more

I took their shilling heedlessly.
My wedding-suit they tore
my love will ne'er again see me.

Our wedding day it was to be
My love fell to the floor
nor will I see her more.

Right from beside my bride-to-be
they seized me just before
My love may ne'er again see me
nor will I see her more.

The Sexy Secretary

Now a girl, being interviewed, shouldn't sit there,
stunning legs in stretch nylons, her ass almost bare,
one foot idly dangling a shoe in the air,
in a posture inviting, that's simply not fair.

For a red-blooded boss finds it hard to resist
the impression she wants to be cuddled and kissed
and, if he doesn't try, he won't know what he's missed
'coz a girl who's neglected gets easily pissed.

You can see that this one is a bit of a flirt,
from the way she's displaying what's under her skirt
and that open-neck blouse doesn't really conceal
two magnificent boobs you'd go giddy to feel.

She can tell, from your looks, that her parts are admired
and is confident she'll be immediately hired.

The Entered Apprentice

He comes in total darkness;
he cannot see the light
for he's completely hoodwinked, quite
without the gift of sight.

His breast is bared to demonstrate
he's not of female sex.
The Junior Deacon guides him through
whatever happens next.

His arm made bare, he's weaponless;
his right heel is slipshod.
He's first expected to confess
a firm belief in God.

The Master poses questions
to which he must reply
before he's obligated,
his fidelity to try.

He swears he'll never willingly
divulge to any other,
the secrets he may henceforth learn
as a Masonic Brother.

Once having sworn with hand upon
The Book of Sacred Law,
his blindfold is removed, that Light
and Sight God may restore.

And now he is enabled to
discover the precepts
on which our Craft is founded -
having taken his first steps.

The Family Test

I was a very happy man. My girlfriend of one year
had just agreed to marry me. None were to me more dear.
The only bother on my mind was her gorgeous younger sister
who seemed to have a crush on me though I seldom touched or kissed her.

She wore tight, skimpy miniskirts but rarely donned a bra.
and, frequently, would turn her back while bending down quite far,
exhibiting right stunning legs for a girl of twenty-two
and underneath her skirt, of which I got a splendid view.

It had to be deliberate when she was near to me
for she never showed to others what she offered me to see.
I must say that I was not averse to taking in the sight
but, on the contrary, enjoyed as often as I might.

One day my girlfriend's sister called and asked if I would come
and check the wedding-list with her while she was all alone.
When I arrived, she whispered in my ear that she had some
hot feelings and desires for me she could not overcome.

She told me that she wanted sex with me, just once, before
I got married to her sister and committed evermore.
This sent me into total shock – I couldn't say a word -
in fact, I scarcely could believe the things that I'd just heard.

She said: "I'm going to my room and, if you want a fling,
just come upstairs and get me – I will give you everything!"
Well, I was stunned - I watched her climb the stairs up to the floor
above, then turned and made a beeline to the exit door.

Outside, at once I headed straight towards my waiting car
and thanked The Lord I didn't have to run so very far.
With sudden shock I realised my future family
were gathered round my car, all joyfully applauding me.

My girlfriend's father hugged me, tears were streaming from his eyes.
He told me I had passed their family test, to my surprise.
He said they could not ask for any better man than me
to be their daughter's husband and to join their family.

I've never told my girlfriend's mother or her dear Papa
how I thank God I always keep my condoms in my car...

Of course I often come across my dear wife's little sister
and wonder how things might've gone if, haply, I'd not missed her.

dedicated with love to my cousin, R. Mark Wyles, who sent me the story which inspired this mini-ballad.

The Night Before Christmas

T'was the night before Christmas and, down at the pub,
which Santa prefers to the gentlemen's club,
the reindeer were having the odd quiet beer
before they set out to dispense Christmas cheer.
Well, they had quite a few and got steadily pissed
and, when he'd had four, Santa mislaid his list
where were written the names of the bad girls and boys
to make sure that he left them no presents or toys.

For as every kid knows (or they bloody well should!)
that unless you've helped mummy and been really good,
when Santa comes round, all his presents to bring,
you're stuffed! The ole bastard won't leave you a thing!
In fact, if you've played up and been really bad,
like prying through keyholes when mum's sucking dad
or letting your friends watch to see your folks screwing
and charging a dollar to watch what they're doing,

or helping yourself to the change from mum's purse
or maybe, some crime that is twenty times worse,
like swearing in Sunday school, playing with yourself,
or dropping your drawers and being caught by an elf,
(for the elves keep a watch on all kids' fun and games
and of those who are naughty, they write down the names),
well, I'm sorry for what Santa leaves you, old chap,
'coz the best you will get is a load of old crap.

But the worst thing about Santa losing his list
is the fact that a lot of 'good' kids will get missed
and some of them have an identical name
so mistakes can occur when a lot are the same.
All these problems are greatly compounded, you see,
'coz the old fella has a piss-poor memory
so the whole distribution becomes hit-and-miss
when he's lost all his records and been on the piss.

Now children, tomorrow when, under the tree,
you find that there aren't many presents to see,
you now know what happened (and it's no use to bawl
because what Santa's left you is sweet bugger all!)
It's not that your parents and Santa were mean
but for reasons I've told you which I hope you've seen
and the whole situation is made doubly sad
if you've been good all year when you could have been bad!

Walk Naked in New Zealand Day

Remember! Mark your calendars! At noon next Saturday,
all patriotic women should walk NAKED round their block
so terrorists who view them, hopefully, drop dead from shock
and you'll have played your part in getting rid of them this way.

You're probably aware that, if a Muslim male should see
a female person naked who is other than his wife,
he is compelled, at once by Shariah law, to take his life
or forfeit any place in Paradise eternally.

If every patriotic Kiwi woman, for one hour,
patrols the streets around her home with nothing on but shoes
and every Kiwi bloke sits in a lawn-chair with his booze
you're showing your support and demonstrating Kiwi-power.

But, if you're far too modest or won't walk because it's wet;
too cowardly or lily-livered to participate,
you're aiding Al Qaeda in their diabolic hate
and, if attacked by jihad, just what you deserve, you'll get.

The NZ Government applauds your undisguised support.
We'll line up in your street, for sport, some terrorists we've caught.

What I Like

I'm often asked if I will tell
about the things I like best. Well,
I love brunettes who doff bikinis
and haven't shaved their in-betweenies

As I'm a PhD you see
in the science of Boobology
I like a girl with well-formed tits
as well as all her other bits
and if she's got a bit of hair
beneath her arms and well down there
I have to tell you I don't care
for shaven legs or anywhere.

From which, I'm sure that you can tell
I like my femmes au naturelle.

First Frost

warm day of summer
unexpected frosty night
freezing chilly morn.

a beautiful summer day and we were caught quite unawares by the cold snap that night brought with hard frost and a drop to 1 degree

A Christmas Gift for a Very Dear Friend

I searched through every stand and stall
To find a Christmas gift for you.
I thought the Market had it all
But nothing there, I saw, would do.

Green jade or paua, bone or wood;
No pendants, bangles, rings or such
That seemed to me were any good….
'Twas not the price – no cost too much.

Glass beads and baubles, gemstones too,
Paintings of scenes and portraits crude,
Pictures of Christchurch, old and new,
Some framed in metal, some in wood;

Hats of pure possum, wool or skin,
Grass skirts or scarves of silk so bright,
Trinkets of silver, pewter, tin -
None that would suit you - none quite right.

So I decided that, instead,
I'd give you something of my own.
Thoughts that were springing from my head;
Feelings that from my heart have grown.

Oh! Leave those tawdry wares behind!
Let them their Market stalls abide!
Take here this verse, straight from my mind
And heart - for YOU... my love beside!

A Highland Lassie's Prayer...

Dear GOD, Creator of the sky and all this land,
I thank Thee, humbly, for my life this morn.
My Sweetheart's far away from where I stand,
Upon this hilltop, gazing at the dawn.

I thank Thee for those golden clouds above,
The snow-capped peaks, the heather'd mountainsides,
The river flowing widely, as Your Love
Will keep him safe wherever he abides.

I thank Thee for the verdant valley grass
And envy not the soaring eagles' view;
For I can pray to You whate'er may pass.
Do eagles, in their flight, consider You?

Lord, let no evil Fate my love befall,
While he is absent faring far away,
Hear my prayer, Lord, and let my call
Grant Thy Enduring Love to him this day.

But if, perchance, Oh Lord, it were Thy Will
That he should perish in some far-off land,
I'd brave the bitter grief that comes to kill
And, dying, I would try to understand.

And, when my span of years will have been spent
If Heav'n holds half the beauty I now see,
I'll come to You and will be well content
If You'll have brought my sweetheart home to me.

A Maytime Sonnet for a Special Friend

Alas, no Mayflow'r nor Hawthorne I find.
Fain would I but a single posy send
To one who is my very special friend.
How could sweet Nature thus be so unkind?

In my whole garden scarce a flower now glows.
The autumn crocus long has gone to bed;
Miniature cyclamen has hid her head;
Nerines and fuschias now are all that shows.

Gone is the summer glory that was ours:
Lilies, camellias, pansies, daisies white:
Lavender, roses, polyanthus bright,
Purple wisteria draped o'er leafy bowers.

Since no May posy can adorn her head -
These Irises I send to her instead.

A Smoker's Lament

I want to give up smoking.
I'm really trying to.
Well, it's an easy thing to say
But a damned hard thing to do.

I've tried out all those patchy things
The oral stuff as well.
They're OK for the first three days
And then I go through Hell!

The doctor's warned me I should stop
The boxes warn me too
With scary message on the top
Saying "Smoking Can Kill You".

Well, I don't want to die just yet
And so I really try.
I've lots and lots of Willpower;
It's of Won'tpower that I'm shy.

I've resolved to stop buying them;
I can't afford the cost.
But then I smoke my "Last one" and
My resolution's lost.

Some people get their joy in life
From cocktails in a bar
For me the supreme pleasure
Is a really fine cigar.

still smoking...

Sequel to "A Smoker's Lament"

It's two weeks since I last had a smoke
The longest durned weeks of my life.
But at least I've made two people happy
My doctor and my darling wife.

They've been at me and at me about it
With a good fifty reasons to stop
Saying it's easy to quit if you want to -
Just you keep well away from that shop.

Well the shop has a new Chinese owner
And I've tried to explain to him twice
That I'm really determined to kick it
Tho' his daughter's so charming and nice.

I'd sneak round to that shop in a minute
Just to buy one more tin, maybe two,
But my friends, one by one, dump me in it
Saying "Gosh we're so proud of you, Hugh."

My special friend says that she's quitting
She is using reduction techniques -
While I am just going "cold turkey"
And I've managed to get through two weeks.

So, my friends, foes and family, forgive me
If I don't seem my usual self
It's the thought of those gorgeous Wee Willems
Sitting unbought, unsmoked on the shelf.

A Timely Lament

When she and I are chatting
My heart's so filled with joy
No matter what we talk about
I'm like a teenage boy!

I rise up bright and early
'Fore any others stir.
For me it is the 'crack of dawn' -
It's afternoon for her.

We live in countries far apart
Time-difference is the crunch.
When I am having breakfast
She's finishing her lunch!

Well, now it's my mid-morning'
I've completed all my chores.
She's taking her pet 'walkies'
Along the dunes and shores.

And worse than that, when I begin
To have MY lunch, you see,
She can't talk then because it's time
For her to cook her tea!!

And when in my mid-afternoon,
A nice chat would be fine,
She's got to go to bed now
'Coz it's getting on for nine!!

I feel so lost and lonely
In these lengthy hours that pall
But I s'pose I should be grateful
That we get to talk at all!!

No wonder that I fill my nights
With whiskies on-the-rocks
While she dreams on towards her dawn.
We're ruled by bloody clocks!!

Then in her early morning
When I am just for bed
I hear her BUZZer warning
And here am I — brain-dead!!

These things are set to try us
Time leads a merry dance.
It's hard, at distance, to conduct
A timed cyber-romance.

A Weather Prayer

Oh GOD who made the Universe,
the Earth, the Sea, the Sky,
Why does it rain in Christchurch so
yet leave Echuca dry?

Why can't the rain fall everywhere.
the sunshine be worldwide
with no more storms or hurricanes,
earthquakes or droughts to ride?

Was Adam's sin so serious,
Eve's punishment so dread
that we must bide this vale of tears
Thy Paradise instead?

My friend Irene is blameless. She
is free of any wrong.
Her little garden thirsts for rain.
Lord, please send some along?

Contemplation

Who is this youth whose face I deem familiar?
Blind recognition, memory's auxiliar...
Was that myself those many years now past
With youthful dreams that, sadly, did not last?
Did all those summers come and pass away
To fade as twilight fades at end of day?

I well recall when I was young and bold
These rushing waters great adventure told.
Heading relentless, swift toward the sea
And unknown future Fate had planned for me.
But now, just like these rocks whereon I stand,
My past is firmly set, future unplanned.

And here, alas, in my declining years
This river that has borne my hopes and fears,
Carries away my seasons one by one
Each ending other, hardly yet begun.
Whereas, in youthful contemplation lost,
I was unable then to reck the cost.

Cyber-Love

I 'met' her on the internet; she sent a note to me
to say she liked my profile and compatibility.
I answered, I was interested and so we made a start
with letters through the dating site. (We lived long miles apart.)
I wanted just a 'pen-pal' with whom I could relate.
She knew that I was married. She was looking for a mate.
We next exchanged addresses, from the dating-site to free
ourselves and start direct Emails between herself and me.

We signed up on the YAHOO! site, bought webcams each in turn,
so we could watch and talk and more about each other learn.
She said one day she loved me. I was "special" to her and,
God help me!, but I fell in love - with her, you understand.
I next arranged to visit her to meet her face-to-face.
She said my wife and I should stay for one week at her place.
Well, I was apprehensive 'cause I wondered when we met
if reality'd be different from the dreams that we had set.

But our visit was a great success - no surprises either way.
I found I loved her more and more with passing of each day.
Then, after we had left her and she next contacted me,
her manner was quite different – cold and distant - do you see?
She said she had a lover she had met some weeks before.
That I was no longer "special" and she loved her new man more.
She said that it was hopeless 'cause of distance and my wife.
She now just wanted me to be a good friend in her life.

Well, I still truly love her. I don't want our talks to end
so I'll eat my pride and hide my love and be her 'cyber-friend'.
And I am really pleased that she has found a lover true.
It's what she wanted, though I think that anyone would do
just as long as they are flesh-and-blood and free to be her mate.
Though I loved her in a cyber way, I see she could not wait.
So be warned all you, my readers, and be sure I tell you dear
that you cannot trust in cyber-love. It may not last the year.

Cyber-Love and Friendship

By chance we've met, on internet, some person quite unknown
and, trying to learn about each other, willingly have shown
our inner secrets – free, as mutual confidence has grown.
Thus our exchanges, one by one, as we each other greet,
flourish in seriousness or fun with emails sharp or sweet.
Would we, I wonder, pass each other unknown in the street?

But cyber, if I may digress, is not an ideal medium
with breakdowns at the server end and other forms of tedium.
Communications falter when they lose synchronization.
and out-of-order messages cause no end of frustration;
or questions stay unanswered while the struggling questionee
is trying to answer number two while you send number three!

It requires a lot of patience, understanding and finesse
to conduct a long- term cyber- relationship.
      Nonetheless
Cyber's the best thing known to date by which we can converse;
without its aid communication could be even worse.
But let's not fool ourselves to thinking we can make a case
for chatting on the internet v. meeting face-to-face.

And if, perchance, a meeting 'in the flesh' can be arranged -
apprehension and anticipation rapidly exchanged -
Will she find me less than handsome?
      Will he find me quite deranged?
When we see each other face to face, no cyber to conceal
all our blemishes and wrinkles from each forehead to each heel,
will we find ourselves upset by what we now see is for real?

Or, because we had a WEBCAM and have seen each other's faces,
is there nothing hidden now between us, nothing that replaces
our dream-constructed images, and all that that implies?
No there isn't - if both parties have refrained from telling lies!
'Coz the meeting in the flesh may lead to stronger love forsooth
if the two of us have always strictly adhered to the truth.

But if one of us has been untrue and falsehoods has expressed
our relationship is doomed to founder, though we try our best.
We may wonder why it's 'going wrong' and why our hopes 'went West'
but those lies are like a virus that will wreck the strongest nest.
So if YOU are on the internet and chatting with a friend,
don't feed out a load of bullshit, buddy – that's the bloody END!!

There are many cyber-friendships that from year to year endure -
friendships without actual meeting that still flourish strong and sure.
There are many happy couples who can tell you that they met
through one of those dating services that cram the internet.
But all of those successes, I assure you (if I must),
were established on foundations of strict HONESTY and TRUST.

Drought in Canterbury

No rain for twenty weeks!
The parched earth shrieks!
Crazed, hollow-ribbed beasts
Stupidly stagger in endless search
For non-existent nourishment and, worse,
Non-existent relief from the endless torture
Of raging, all-consuming thirst!

Snagging their hooves in the cracked earth.
Stumble, collapse and lie, too enfeebled to rise,
Under the shimmering, furnace-heated skies.
Ten thousand corpses covered with millions of buzzing flies.

Fire danger is extreme! It only needs one spark, one careless match
To initiate a conflagration which the gusting nor-west winds
Spread for miles, consuming dry grass, scrub, timber and
The piles of bloated dead. Flames fanned
By their own heat, hungrier than the dead were,
Devour whatever stands before their unrelenting path
Of unrestrained destruction.

Only the blackened earth remains,
Studded with charred skeletons of former trees,
Twisted fences and the gutted frames of former habitations.
No rain for twenty weeks!

Guests

Ours is a rather tiny home; it's fine just for us two,
With spacious lounge and music room (Piano and Hi-fi too.)
The dining area's open and the kitchen's just beyond
With ample, roomy cupboard space (of cooking we're both fond.)

But there's a problem that we face when people come to stay.
We only have one spare bedroom (With just us, that's Okay.)
I use it as my study, it's lined with tapes and books;
My puter's on a desk in there and very nice it looks.

We have a drop-down couch and when a guest is sleeping there
We pump a mattress up, real hard. (It's comfy, so I hear.)
The problem is when people come and they are here to stay,
I have to clear my "rubbish" out and store it all away.

We have a roomy cellar, down "below stairs", understand?
My stuff gets stored in there each time we have a house-guest land.
Well, our guests are very welcome because we love them so.
We love to have them with us and we love them when they go!

We both say (when they've gone) that it was nice to have them here
But ain't it nice for just us two and now my study's clear.
So now my real problem starts and this I really mind.
The stuff that I had stored below I simply cannot find!

Happy Heart

Happy the Heart that's full of LOVE;
Under no burden of Envy nor Lust,
Greed nor Grief nor gnawing Jealousy,
Hate nor Despair nor Covetousness,
Selfishness nor Blind Deception.

Happy the Heart that's full of HOPE,
Empty of Evil, devoid of Doubt,
Amply filled with CHARITY,
Resting in FAITH in the Lord.
Try me Father and grant mine Thy Everlasting
                GRACE!

         Amen.

How Are You Today?

When I ever ask that question,
Like "How are you today?",
I am always rather nervous
that the questionee will say
"I'm not well you know" and then I'm trapped
and cannot get away.

Happy Mother's Day

Last night we entertained
a couple of friends for dinner.
The wife had just farewelled her son.
He has gone to Iraq.
He will be working (non-army)
for the British Government
as a bodyguard.
He will earn over $NZ1,000.00
for every day that he works.
If he is killed, his next-of-kin (partner)
will get a lump payout (68,000 Pounds).
(How much is his life worth?)

His mother could not stop him going.

HAPPY MOTHER'S DAY, N...

And a quiet thought for all mothers
who have sons (or daughters) in Iraq.

If Ever...

If ever you should need me
That need I'd understand
Your call I'd promptly answer
And wait your next command.

Your tears reach out and call me
O'er miles of sea and sand
Oh would I speed swift to your side
Perchance to hold your hand.

Would, in my presence, you could find
Some rest, some peace, some calm,
Some confidence, some peace of mind
And all-pervading balm.

Anxieties of yesterday,
The troubles of tomorrow
Like phantom wraiths would fade away.
No pain, no tears, no sorrow.

But differences of time, my love,
And distance 'tween our shores
Keep you apart from my side and
Prevent me reaching yours.

I can't attain you physically;
My strength's of no avail.
I only can advise and listen
To your anguished tale.

Oh, you can pour out all your mind
And I will understand,
But problems just related are,
To me, not quite first-hand.

If cyber weren't available
We never would have known
Each other nor would we be friends
As close as we have grown.

So though I can't be near to you
To counsel, pray or plan,
I hope to give some cyber-help
And comfort where I can.

If I Am Allowed

If I Am Allowed.

If I am allowed only one Love, let it be for GOD;
For, through loving GOD, I can love my fellow-man.

If I am allowed only one Hope, let it be for Peace;
For, with Peace, GOD's Love can prevail.

If I am allowed only one Belief, let it be in GOD;
For, in believing, I may have Everlasting Life.

If I am allowed only one Faith, let it be in myself;
For, if I have Faith, I shall see GOD.

Mammoth Lovesong

If you were a lady mammoth (and that would enlarge your stature!)
Well, I wouldn't go round spanking you 'coz that is not my nature.
But if I was a mammoth too I could not guarantee
That I wouldn't want to 'bonk' you - that is natural, you see.

And we might have baby mammoths - little woolly, cuddly things
And just think of all the mammoth joy that having babies brings.
And although you say that spanking makes a woman feel "free"
I can't believe a female mammoth really would agree.

But all this is just my dreaming after your amusing poem
If you don't want my attentions you can tell me to go home.
But I'll hang around, old tho' I am, and worship from afar
'Cause, Aimee, you are booful and I love you as you are!

Inspiration

I want to write some music
Coz the notes are in my head,
Nagging, begging to be written
So in turn they can be read.

But the harmony, tho' waiting,
I just cannot get quite right.
Oh it's all so damn frustrating
And I've been up half the night.

The melody is clear enough
The chords are not so clear.
I've changed them over twenty times.
They're still not right, I fear.

I'm sick of it already,
And I want to go to bed.
Can't keep my pencil steady
And I've almost lost the thread.

I did want to write this music
Coz the notes were in my head.
Well, they'll have to bloody stay there
I'll just write this poem instead.

Irrevocable Time

Our loving was pure rapture
As she gave herself to me.
Oh! GOD! Let me recapture
That split infinity!
I lost myself inside her
My climax so intense
I couldn't understand her words -
They didn't make much sense.
But then her message dawned on me;
She spoke about this other
That she was going away with soon -
For months he'd been her lover.
This was her final time with me
I'd never see her more……..
The axe was lying close to hand
Upon the dusty floor.
I snatched it, blindly struck her once
Full force into her face
It clove her features in - blood
Spurting all over the place……
She staggered out into the night;
Fell lifeless to the ground.
Her screams died out - I never will
Forget that dreadful sound.
(They always said my sudden rage
Would cause somebody's death.)
If I could just return the page -
Retrieve the past beneath……..
Oh! GOD! YOU are OMNIPOTENT!!
Creator of all men!!
Turn Time back just ten minutes, please!
We were still lovers then!!

Jack the Ripper

T'were in the merry month of May
In eighteen eighty eight
Emerged in good old London Town
A monster foul, though quite unknown,
A legend to this day.

Dubbed 'Jack the Ripper', he's come down
An unsolved mystery.
His victims prostitutes all were
But everybody lived in fear.
He terrorised the Town.

From midnight until six o'clock
At weekends round Whitechapel
He'd stalk his victims (lonely hookers,
some of whom were quite good lookers).
They did NOT die from shock.

He strangled them and then he slit
Their throats. There's worse to tell.
He cut their bellies open wide
And sometimes slashed from side to side
Then hacked their sexual bit.

From some he took the heart or spleen,
Their kidneys or their liver;
From some removed the uterus....
How came among the rest of us
A monster so obscene?

Their mutilated bodies lay
Blood-spattered in the gutters.
Victorian police weren't skilled
Enough to find out who had killed
So many in this way.

Butcher or lunatic or surgeon?
They never could discover.
Corpses they found but nothing more;
The only thing they knew for sure -
None of those dead was virgin.

A Pub sign's now the epitaph
To mark this sorry tale.
I tell it not from morbid vanity
But 'coz this contest's run by SANITY
Who's looking for a laugh!!!

Love Poems for the Sick

Why are love-poems so often deadly serious?
Why are nearly all the love-ballads so sad?
Their rampant morbidity is hilarious
And, which is worse, the standard is so bad!

I'm sick of broken hearts and love rejected,
Of suicidal outbursts and the rage
Of unrequited love or unsuspected
Jealous tantrums no excuses can assuage.

On the other hand, I'm also tired of hearing
All that slush about the purity of love
How the souls extol, the hearts are ever bearing
Adoration for men sent from heaven above.

And I utterly deplore those graveyard blunders
Or the overstated Valentinian mush
Or celestial calls to Nature and her Wonders
Written 'specially for Contests in a rush.

Why does every f......g mediocre 'poet'
Writing hackneyed, clichéd phrases by the mile
Get applauds from commenters who think they 'know it'
Irrespective of the content or the style?

Oh! Some greater mind than mine already stated
That acrostic poems as tributes are so sweet
But their value has been highly over-rated
As the writer and the writee rarely meet.

So let's have a great poetic revolution
Sweep the sand, to coin a phrase or make a point,
Let some rising genius offer a solution
To the problems that leave noses out of joint.

Me and My Muse

I've never actually seen her but
I've felt her loving hands.
She leans upon my shoulder; right
behind me's where she stands.

She brings the scents of Nature;
She brings the sounds of sea;
She brings all sorts of visions bright
And feeds them all to me.

She tells me tales of long ago;
Of folk and faery lore;
Of knights and lovely ladies
From romances long before.

She tells me of her travels.
Countries far and wide she's seen
And she leaves me with these longings to
go back to where she's been.

She tells me great love-stories.
Sad, ill-fated or sublime.
But also tells of feuds and wars
That happen all the time.

She takes me to the Heavens;
Shows me all the mystery
Of stars and planets, endless space
And university.

She guides my thoughts so gently,
Sometimes serious, often fun
And helps me when I'm helpless
To pursue what I've begun.

She makes it seem quite easy
To translate my thoughts to verse.
When she's with me it just flows free,
When she's gone, there's nothing worse.

She doesn't come at bidding;
She won't appear at will.
You may think that I am kidding
If I say I love her still.

Her soul is full of Beauty.
Her heart is full of Love.
Her mind is full of Knowledge.
She's from God, in Heav'n above.

She taught me about CHARITY;
With HOPE my heart she filled;
Inspired my soul with FAITH and former
fears and doubts she stilled.

I think she wears a robe of white
With sandals on her feet...
Whatever, she's the loveliest creature
I shall ever meet.

So whatever you want written
About Earth, or Sea, or Sky,
Or Love, we'll write a poem for you,
My lovely Muse and I.

Message for the Upper Class

You were born to lots of money;
You don't have to work a job;
You can live on cream and honey.
Why be such a bloody snob?

All those years in school together
When I helped you with your swot;
Now you don't know even whether
You should say "hello" or not.

There's been quite a few occasions
When chance might have had us meet
But, 'coz of our diff'rent stations,
You just walked across the street.

Well I don't assume an accent
That is 'lah-de-dah' like yours
And, in spite of your so-called "descent",
We still call you "Droopy Drawers".

There's another thing I'll tell you
Tho' this may make you quite sore,
There are some could buy or sell you.
You are just a f.....g bore!

Can you hear a Mozart Symphony
With much greater joy than me?
Do you laugh and think it funny
If somebody farts at tea?

Do you get up really early -
See the sun come up at dawn
Or just sulk in bed, all surly,
Till you've wasted half the morn?

Can you read a sad quatroon
And sense the tragedy beneath?
I would take your silver f…..g spoon
And shove it through your teeth!

You think you're the cat's pyjamas
Just because you're "upper class".
Take your plane to the Bahamas
And then stick it up your arse!!

Midnight Waiter's Blues

I'm sat here at my computer if you guys can just believe it.
I've a hundred other things to do but I'm too scared to leave it.
She said before she signed off "Maybe I will come on later"
But she never gave me any time so I am just a "waiter".

My Yahoo's running, sound is on, I'm terrified becuz,
If I fall asleep, when she comes back I might not hear her BUZZ!
And though, as far as she's concerned, I can wait here all day
If I don't respond immediately to her there's hell to pay.

And every other minute I must check my Inbox and
AP in case Emails or IM's she decides to send.
God knows it's past my bedtime and the timeclock slowly creeps
While I wonder what the time is over there and when SHE sleeps.

After midnight now and everybody here has gone to bed
And the whole world all around me is as quiet as though it's dead.
I now estimate the time there must be five or six a.m.
But I have to check again to see if there's a "Here I Am!"

Well, the Inbox says "No Messages", AP has nothing new;
So I switch back to Yahoo to see if anything's come through.
But the Yahoo "Friends' List" shows that there is NOBODY on-line.
She's forgotten me! I'm off to bed!... and ain't life bloody fine?

My Heart is like a Mansion

My heart is like a mansion
With many rooms to spare.
The biggest room is for my wife
She's safe forever there.

Another room is for my GOD,
My kids and parents too.
My dead grandparents have their room,
And rellies (if they knew).

Well, I am a Freemason.
I've been Lodge Master twice.
We practice Love, Fraternity
And Truth – avoiding Vice.

And I am now Lodge Chaplain
With all that post assumes.
My love extends to all my friends.
(Can always add more rooms!)

Lord JESUS said, while on this Earth,
To those prepared to hear:
"My Father's House has many mansions –
I will lead you there."

Yes, my heart's like a mansion.
Each room is filled with love
And there's a special room for YOU –
Just as GOD's Heaven above.

My Last Day

Well, I won't waste time having a shower;
The milk I'll leave down at the gate;
If you'd hoped to make me a teetot'ler
You will find that you're too bloody late.

Gonna walk to MacDonalds' for breakfast;
Have a Big Mac an' coke an' lots more;
Spill tomato sauce over the table
An' throw chips all over the floor.

Gonna get in my rusty jalopy;
Got no warrant? I don't give a shit.
Gonna drive the wrong way up the one-ways
And give other drivers a fit.

Gonna crawl along slow in the fast lane
And speed up at dangerous bends;
Overtake on the yellow "don't cross" lines;
Pay no heed where the speed limit ends.

I'll ignore all the peak rush-hour traffic;
Never look before I drive across
Nor pay any attention to red lights;
Park in "Disabled" zones. What's the loss?

Crash the queue at the fast check-out counters
An' have more than ten things in "EXPRESS".
Buy up hugely in smokes, wine an' choc'late
An' leave all their neat shelves in a mess.

Gonna bust or at least mutilate
Every damn parking meter I see;
Kick every sign into the gutter;
Go wherever, when I wanna pee.

I will not pay my overdue taxes.
I will not pay my regular dues.
Put all unpaid bills out with the rubbish
Which includes the accounts for my booze.

Throw the rubbish right over my back fence;
On your neat bloody lawn it can stay.
My doggy will crap on your garden
An' I'll just walk, laughing, away.

I'll leave empties all over your driveway;
Pull your gate off, lean it on your fence;
Put your garbage can right in the middle
Where you'll hit it at night, causing dents.

Then, maybe, you'll at last get the message
When my friendship you try to pursue,
That I don't need no good f......g neighbours.
Where I'm going I won't THINK of you!

On my very last evening I'll open
All my windows and party all night
An' I'll drink myself under the table
An' then just go out like a light.

The hi-fi I'll leave on at its loudest -
Rowdy music that's got real stomp
And I'll blast the whole district to bedlam;
Make my last day one hell of a romp!!!

An' I'll write me one long final poem
With no metre or pauses or rhyme;
Use the filthiest words I can muster
An' give AP one helluva time!

In my lifetime I hardly was noticed.
I was often completely ignored.
Well, in death I will sure be remembered
As the guy who went right overboard!!!

Old Age Despair

What good the golden hoard, the noble fame
Of heroes or the praise of younger Man?
The hand of Death makes Man but a mere name
And none may linger longer than the span
Of years which fickle Fate allots.

We start to die when we begin to live.
The ages pass and we and all our kin
Are dead and those who died can only give
Scant recompense for all we did. Oh! What a sin
To live at all. Our whole life rots!

Is there a God who looks upon our toil?
Does He not watch our progress and approve
Our every act? Are we but soil
That lie beneath this Earth never to move?
Man dies when he is dead and ties the knots
Around him in the silent graveyard plots.

On LOVE and HUGS

I had this irate husband
Who emailed me today
Saying "Why do you put 'Love and Hugs'
On everything you say?"

"You said it to my wife, mate,
And now I'm in the poo.
She says I never tell HER that.
It's all because of you!"

Well, it's not on everything, mate,
That this chap, Hugh Wyles, sends.
It's only to my favourites -
My very special friends.

And only to the female ones -
Oh! Never to the men
Or they might think I'm 'queer' or 'gay' -
Only six out of ten.

You see, I LOVE my favourites,
And of their pics I've seen,
I'd really LOVE to HUG them.
So don't work up your spleen!

Your wife's a special person
From everything I know
About her but we haven't got
"A going thing", you know.

And let me tell you matey, while
You're trying to slap my wrist
You may be right annoyed with me
But there's no need to get pissed.

My greetings are quite innocent
As God's in heaven above.
My "LOVE and HUGS" means nothing more
Than good old cyber-love.

I hope I have convinced you,
And nothing you now bugs.....
'Coz I'll keep on loving favourites
And sending LOVE and HUGS!

Sequel to "On LOVE and HUGS"

Well, I'll be damned and jiggered!
Guess what happened here today,
The Bloody phone's been going red-hot
With hubs (and boyfriends!) shooting snot
At all the innocent things I say.
Just look at what it's triggered!

I can say on the other hand
That I'm comforted no end
By nice things that my readers write -
(Some, in the middle of the night.)
They know I've no wish to offend
Or in the crap to land!!

But these demented halfwits who
Have bugged me all day long,
Won't listen to my reasoning,
Don't even spare the seasoning,
Let fly without a prayer or song
I've a message got for you!

Just let me tell you buggers true
If you can curb your dander,
If YOU Loved and Hugged YOUR better half,
You'd be living off the fatted calf.
What's good for goose is good for gander
And so I say F... U!!!

with LOVE and HUGS to ALL my female faves

Our Vanishing Friends

Can't imagine what that trinket you are wearing might have cost.
Do you realise, to own it, that a noble life was lost?
D'you condone disgraceful plunder of the Most Magnificent One
And the most unique of God's creatures that walk beneath His sun?

Was it really worth the price you paid to finance such a sin?
What did jumbo ever do to you that want to kill his kin?
Leave his carcass to hyaenas while his ivory tusks are poached?
Don't you realise humane and legal rules are thereby broached?

Let their ivory rest in Africa. Don't take any away
For the cost is far too high and we must just refuse to pay.
As the rhino once was hunted for it's aphrodisiac' horn,
It is now a sad fact that their population's nearly gone.

While friends may admire your trinket that you wear with such aplomb,
I can't help but think of all the slaughter, adding to the sum
Of Man's callous inhumanity, that's so directly linked
To demise of all the species that have now become extinct.

Past Loves

Where did those youthful passions go?
The laughter and the pain,
The joys, the thrills of years gone by
That never come again?

What happened to those lovely girls
That I once dared to woo?
Have they all married other men?
Do they remember too?

I loved them once so totally;
Each meant the world to me
But their love wasn't strong like mine
They were so fancy free.

And are they now just memories
That slumber in my mind?
When I am gone and think no more,
Will they be left behind?

Those past loves that I once adored;
It makes me feel quite rotten.
Their faces I can still recall
But names I've quite forgotten!

Patience... Impatience

I wait for her BUZZ;
Watching my YAHOO window.
She'll surely call soon?

Maybe she's asleep;
Maybe she's forgotten me.
Maybe she won't call.

I'll wait ten minutes.
Maybe that's not long enough.
Twenty minutes then.

Nope. Still no nothing.
Guess I just keep on waiting.
(In Japanese style?)

Shit! I fell asleep.
How can all that time have passed?
Still she hasn't called.

I can't wait longer.
It's more than a whole hour now.
She can go to Hell!!!

Puter Blues

I'm faced with sheer disaster,
Absolute calamity.
I don't know how I can survive
This dread catastrophee.

My 'puter's on the blink again
It's driving me quite nuts
'Coz everything I try to do
Just kicks me in the guts.

My chat friends I can't contact,
Emails can't read or send,
Yahoo won't even register,
AP's half round the bend.

"Program is not responding";
"Page cannot be displayed"
The 'hourglass' sits there motionless
And won't change, I'm afraid.

I'll have to call the experts in
At ninety bucks a visit
'Coz without a healthy 'puter
Life's just not worth living - is it?

Qui pro Patria necavi sunt

The sod lies still in distant fields
Beneath a foreign sky
Where slumber those who in the throes
Of war 'gainst unknown, alien foes
Left home and heart... to die.

Their slayers had no grievous hate,
No bitter grudge, that they
Should spread the soil with Mothers' toil –
A nation's lifeblood thus despoil
And unknown victims slay.

Some small dictator's blinding greed
Inflamed their nation's pride.
Some doctrine sour did, with the hour,
Become a vengeful lust for power...
So our Youth fought... and died.

They fought for all that we had held
And, at their comrades' side,
Afar and near, without a tear,
Holding their country's freedom dear,
A horde of heroes died.

The Legend of Robin Hood

In Sherwood forest dwelt a man (how well do I proclaim?)
'E'w're known as ROBIN HOOD but, really, Locksley was 'is name.
'E stole from rich to give to poor and on that fact I'll stand.
'E'w're right good man and wot is more, finest archer in the land.

'Tw're in the days of 'Bad King John' (You've 'eard o' MAGNA CARTA'?)
Well, 'e appointed bad sheriffs – but that was just a starter.
One sheriff (I forget 'is name but 'e w're based in Nottingham)
Tried to stop Robin killing game an' set out, bent on swatting 'im.

But Robin were too smart for 'im an' with 'is Merrie Men,
'E copped the sheriff several times then copped 'im once again.
An' in 'is band o' Merrie Men it chanced by sheer good luck
There 'appened a retired monk. 'Is name w're Friar Tuck.

Well, one day Robin was a'restin', sat beneath a tree
'An 'e spies this bird Maid Marion. "Ho Ho! Ha Ha!" says 'e.
So 'e calls on ('oo – you guessed it!) this fat feller, Friar Tuck
'An 'e says "Now varlet, marry us – then I can 'ave a ####"

Well, that is NOT 'ow sex came to be (tho' Maid Marion w're good lookin')
But she got 'er share an', in the meantime she did all the cookin'.
An' wot I've told yer, tho' legend, is dead true fer a starter.
RH, MM, an' the Merrie Men lived 'app'ly ever arter.

Robin Hood - The Final Shot

Now Robin 'ood w'rn't very well.
Bin sinkin' fas' f'r days.
Breathin' 'ard an' weak as 'ell
'Is def'nit fyn'l phase.

The Merrie Men all 'ung aroun';
Maid Marian w're th're too.
Not IN 'is bed! ROUN' it, yer clown!
(All knew Rob's hours w're few.)

Will Scarlett 'e w're there o' course,
As allus, clad in red.
An' Friar Tuck an' Rob's ol' 'orse;
They walked with silent tread.

The sheriff, 'e w're NOT there. 'E
W're otherwise detained.
'E sent a nice 'pology, sayin'
'Is ankle 'e 'ad sprained.

Well bugger me if Robin
Didn't sit up in 'is bed!
'E struggled up, mos' manfully,
An' this 're wot 'e said:

"Fetch me my longbow Friar Tuck!
Give me an arrer too!
Open the winder wide an' I
Will fire that arrer through.

"An' where that arrer lands my friends
'Tis where I'll buried be.
Now stop yer snivellin' all you lot
An' jes' pay 'eed t' me."

So sayin' 'e fell back in bed
An' gasped as if t' croak.
Deep moved they w're, but off they sped
To do wot 'e 'ad spoke.

They found 'is trusty longbow,
Arrers found they th're beside.
They 'anded 'em to Friar Tuck
'an threw t'winder wide.

They lifted poor ole Robin up
An' 'eld 'im sittin' where
'E could look out through t' winder
T'ward Sherwood Forest there.

Tuck placed t' longbow in 'is 'ands
'e placed an arrer too
An', though Rob's 'ands were tremblin' bad,
That mighty bow 'e drew.

Cold sweat stood art upon 'is brow
but 'is spirit still w're strong
an', with 'eroic effort, e'
aimed careful, slow an' long.

'E fired t' arrer in t' air;
T' shaft flew true an' fast.
Took bloody hours t' find it.
(Robin 'ood 'ad breathed 'is last.)

Maid Marian w're right upset
An' so w're Friar Tuck.
Will Scarlett too an' Merrie crew
Felt real down on they'r luck.

So if y're in t' district
An' yer wan'ter find out where
That arrer landed. Sherwood Forest?
No use lookin' there!

Jes' go up t' yon castle an'
(from truth I've never varied)
Look up on top o' t'wardrobe, lad,
'Coz that's where Rob is buried.

Sad Loss

Oh! Wretched morning!
My good friend of threescore years
Died during the night.

Oh! My dear, dear friend!
Why could you not wait for me?
Were you in such haste?

As with every death
This world becomes emptier.
You leave a big void.

Swan Song

I am a white swan,
Flying, neck outstretched,
Soaring on the wind,
The sun on my back,
There is the lake below
Where I will land and meet my mate.

I see her squatting on our nest.
I glide in, folding my wings as I prepare to land.
What was that sudden, loud explosion?
Tearing pain... then numbness...
Why am I falling?... I can't fly...
...the sun has gone out...

On the Death of a Real Poet

He's gone! We may not see his like again.
Yesterday he lived. Today he's freed from pain.
Sickness no more his failing spirit shall assail.
His humour, love, beliefs and writings ever now prevail.
All those who by his teachings set great store
And loved him then, now love him even more.

Many who, while he lived, gave seldom thought
To what he said or wrote or, by his writings, taught
Now, when bereft, make overt, loud complaint
And mourn his passing as a virtual saint.
Haply his writings now they'll read, though late.
Such, I'm afraid, is many a poet's fate.

inspired by the recent death of Repomen79

Story of a Double-Wash!

I did two loads of washing
And hung it all to dry.
A gentle breeze was blowing and
The whole line was quite gently fanned,
The sun shone in the sky.

A flock of bloody seagulls
Flew, crying, overhead.
They dive-bombed half my wash and then
Just circled round and bombed again.
Can any more be said?

Then I looked out my window
The sky was darker now.
A sudden heavy shower of rain
The first in WEEKS!! Christ!! What a pain!
I'll have to do the wash again!
A perfect, bloody cow!

The Rubaiyat of a Fallen Pear

If I were a pear and I lay in the grass
I would never know whether my face or my ass
Was turned upwards and sunwards or down to the ground
So I'd lie there unmoving nor make any sound.

And in hot summer sunshine the wasps would soon come
And would busily munch at the base of my bum;
They would chew through my coat and crawl under my skin
Leaving holes in my sides to show where they have been.

I'd give all of my flesh to the sparrow or thrush
Or the starling or blackbird who eat of my mush
And the blowflies would buzz me and land in my rot
But I'd lie there unmoving and never wot not.

I would lie there, quite helpless, by night and by day
Getting lesser and less as I'm eaten away.
Until final oblivion helps me to pass
Through the pear-ly pink gates of a fat earthworm's arse.

The Self-made Nerd

I frequently declaim at home
Macaulay's "Lays of Ancient Rome"
and you could very well hear me
reciting Gray's great "Elegy".
If that is not enough for you
I'll do the "Kama Sutra" too
and just for extra impact's sake
my Shakespeare is a piece of cake.
The whole of Palgrave's Treasury,
th'entire Medical Diction'ry,
I can repeat at drop of hat
and you should hear my "Rubaiyat"!
I've memorised Vergil and Homer,
Caesar I can recite at will.
Any Masefield "Salt Sea Poem" or
Newbold trilogy I'll kill.
I also conjugate with ease
the latin names of shrubs and trees
or, I can tell you without pause
full genera of dinosaurs.
If stars or planets cause you trouble,
I'll list all those now seen by Hubble.
Phonebooks I can repeat at random;
Encyclopaedias quote in tandem
and, for amusement, I'm quite liable
to itemize the Holy Bible.
My IQ's high as Wiz of OZ
(but can't remember what that was.)
What I cannot now comprehend,
(perhaps I'm slightly round the bend?)
is why the folks who used to know me
avoid me now...
Please, someone, show me?

Things to Come

Oh God! Creator of the Earth, the Sky,
The Heavens and all Life.
You watch with Your All-Seeing Eye
This world of pain and strife.

Who gave to Man the Freedom
To choose, to plan his acts
Yet gave him not the wisdom
To contemplate the facts.

"Can You forgive me?" if I pray
And, in this year ahead,
"I can't stop crying" for the way
This World is being led?

Must Man be so forgetful
Of Thy Son Jesus' Word?
Or Allah's plea, so fretful now.
May Peace be on us Lord?

Lord, "Please don't close Your Eyes" to us,
This world, this humankind.
May Love increase and bring us Peace
And War, Disease and Famine cease
And in this coming year release
"Something worth leaving behind".

To All My (Female) Favourites

As the column that I started (you'll recall, "On LOVE and HUGS")
Has been closed (and hopefully my lines are now swept under rugs).
There are some more things I want to say to you while I'm intact
So please read this message carefully – it's plain, unvarnished fact.

You have probably deduced by now from what I say and write,
That I've grown immensely fond of you. I don't know if it's right
For a seventy-two year male to cyber-love nice girls like you,
When he's married. Might not seem a very proper thing to do!

But whatever people say about it, I don't care a jot.
For the fact is, you are such a veritably gorgeous lot!
Any bloke with red blood in his veins is certainly aware
That to have so many new girl-friends is beyond one man's fair share!

Now I hope that what I've said above won't make you think I'm greedy
Or that I am kinky, twisted or perhaps a trifle needy.
I'm completely sane and pretty sound (despite a smoker's cough)
And I want to make a promise to you all, ere you run off.

Ev'ry morning bright and early 'fore the day's work has begun
I will boot up my PC and when it's going, 'up and run',
I'll go straight into the AP site and login, then I'll go
To the 'Latest By My Favourites', because I love you so.

I will then inspect your IM's and your Emails at my leisure
And your comments on MY poetry, which give me so much pleasure.
And, in a happy frame of mind, I'll then review your work.
(So I'll hope there isn't too much sad and gloomy stuff or murk.)

Then to each of you I'll comment in my usual kindly way
And I hope that what I say to you will really make your day.
But if I have to be truthful and my criticism bugs
I will sign my comment anyway "Hugh Wyles, with LOVE and HUGS".

Now, my favourites who are masculine I must not disregard.
They will get the same fair treatment though I sometimes find it hard.
For if men write poetry, that's good, and tho' some may be bards,
They won't get kisses or "Love and Hugs", they'll just get "Kind Regards".

And I want to thank all those of you who sent such lovely pics.
I'm so glad you liked your poems, (you're a lovely bunch of chicks.)
To the ones who've not sent photos yet, you've still a running chance,
But you probably won't get an invitation to the dance.

Well, I've finished now. I have to go and check my morning's mail.
Then I must report-in promptly, coz I'm only out on bail.
If you write me love-poems, please make sure they're not beyond the pale.
Want you ALL to be my Valentine. I'LL SEE YOU ALL IN JAIL!!!

To My Son, With Love

Love's not a finite thing, my son.
It's not kept in a can.
Your love for Nature, Beauty, Grace
And for your Fellow-Man
Is boundless. If your Heart allows
Your feelings to run free,
Your love for GOD is endless, son,
As I hope it is for me.

Some day you'll meet a woman, son,
I hope it will be soon.
You'll marry her and love her dear
As stars all love the moon.
You'll promise to be faithful
By the Lord of Heaven above,
But you, my son, can never give
One person ALL your love.

Just look to JESUS' teaching, son,
The Bible makes it clear
and "Love thy neighbour as thyself"
"Hold every creature dear".
Yet "Covet not thy neighbour's wife,
His servant nor his beast".
If you keep those commandments, son,
You'll be content at least.

So, son, I hope you're listening
While I can tell you straight
That Love is spirit-healing, son,
The opposite is Hate.
Love all your friends, your relatives,
Your wife, your kids and you
Will be a happy man, my son,
And you will be rich too!

Aussie Boobs

Sir David Peter Robertson once, boastfully, declared
that Aussie sheilas have the finest tits
and here are two examples which are beautifully paired,
that show his claim appropriately fits.

Now both these girls are known to me as typical young mothers
and, internationally, I'm sure that they
would 'Advance Australia Fair' in world contests against all others
and, unlike cricketers, would win the day.

If I were asked to judge these two, I'd say the pair at left
would surely win the "Neatest Booby" prize
with extra points awarded for her captivating cleft;
while the other might pick up a few for size.

That I'm partial to Australian boobs, I freely make admission
and I'm grateful I can show these with the owners' kind permission.

More on Boobs
some advice to students

Most know that I'm a boobaphile
who readily will run a mile
to study what I love the best:
a proud, curvaceous female chest.
Few things can beat a pair of boobs
with no sharp corners as in cubes.

Boobs tend to come in different sizes
and often cause acute surprises
for some are so minutely small,
they're hardly worth a look at all
while others, stunningly immense,
astound the eye and numb the sense.

Some, self-sustaining, prance and perk;
some wobble, bounce, cavort or jerk.
With ageing most will tend to droop
and hang loose when their owners stoop.
Whatever shape is most appealing
they're all magnificent for feeling.

A lot of money has been spent
to find the ideal measurement.
Some women hope for increased sizes
from set aerobic exercises
while others make us look askance
at their enormous breast implants.

But the best boobs will always be
the ones developed naturally
while pairs most pleasing to the eyes
are those which are of matching size.
and often it improves the scene
if there's a yawning cleft between.

Of mother nature's many treats
it's hard to beat two well-formed teats
especially displayed at best
being mounted on abundant breast.
Sometimes, when prominent and pert,
they show well through a tight T-shirt.

Boobography, while not exact,
requires a fair amount of tact.
The serious boobographer
would never get to see a pair
if, gauchely crude and lacking wits,
his opening line's: "Let's see yer tits!"

The serious student, 'ere he works,
will view far more mammiferous perks
if his approach he first refines,
developing his opening lines.
The soft, persuasive word will stand
in better stead than harsh command.

Some willing women freely show
what nature did on them bestow
while others, modest, prim or shy,
will sock a student in the eye.
This constant element of danger
exists if you arouse their anger.

But let's assume that, haply, you
are ready to enjoy the view.
Either alone, or with a buddy,
a woman's breasts you get to study.
Do NOT be tempted, as you might,
in any way to pinch or bite!

Remember that the female gender,
the epitome of body splendour,
requires, of males, respect to render,
for women's boobs are somewhat tender.
If you, unwittingly, cause hurt
you may not get beneath her shirt.

From personal experience
it's best to use one's common sense
and women often best respond
to some expensive restaurant
where their permissiveness may well
depend upon the size of bill.

I hope these words of admonition
explain the difficult position
and guide the would-be student while,
perfecting a persuasive style,
he studies, fervently like me,
the science of Boobography.

More Still on Boobs
a more advanced Study Paper

I've now attained my PhD
in science of Boobology
which is a more advanced Degree
than basic straight Boobography.

Because I've always been alert
I've now become somewhat expert
in study of the female breast;
that veritable 'treasure-chest'.

In many countries, far and wide,
hundreds of women's boobs I've eyed,
'most every shade and colour seen:
white, yellow, brown, black, red or green.

At shows, I've judged all shapes and sizes,
awarding ribbons, cups and prizes.
When singling out a champion pair,
I'm always rigorously fair.

I've also seen amazing sights
in bras, bikinis, thongs or tights
and oft', in cooler months, a bumper
in tight T-shirt or woolly jumper.

In places most men fear to tread;
in boudoir, bower, bath or bed,
abundant boobs may best be found
by those who search and feel around.

They don't just pop up when they're bidden
and often they're discreetly hidden
but, to the well-trained, practiced eye,
their presence is not hard to spy.

Observed on land or underwater,
I've seen boobs where one didn't oughter;
in changing rooms and under showers
through keyholes where I've watched for hours.

(Not for my own self-satisfaction
or even from innate attraction
but 'dans la devouee etude'
of female bosoms a la nude.)

While some men study legs or calves
I concentrate on upper halves.
Though not ignoring eyes and faces
I gravitate to lower places.

I seldom go below the waist.
(It's all a matter of good taste)
Though one does find attractive places
when delving in those lower spaces.

But my advice to all you dudes
who genuinely study boobs
is: "Keep your mind on where you're at
and don't forsake the tit for tat!"

More Boob Experiences
adult and personal

I hope that, by relating personal experience,
I won't cause any one of you discomfort or offence.
I have certain of my students who are always, curiously,
wanting to hear some of the things that have befallen me.

Well, as one travels round the world and grapples with surprises
encountering a great variety of shapes and sizes,
one finds they range from skinny to obese, some merely fatter
and one soon learns that creed and colour really doesn't matter.

It is a well-known fact that, round the ancient world of former times,
most women went bare-breasted even in the cooler climes.
Of course Neanderthals who wore no singlets, bras or vests
were known to have exceptionally broad and hairy chests.

And hirsute bosoms really, I reluctantly must say,
are viewed as unconventional in fashion fields today;
so he who wants to specialise in boobs with lots of hair
should study in Sumatra (orang-utans' native lair.)

Boobs v. Books

I'm asked why now, instead of boobs, I'm writing about books
and whether, in the sear of life, boobs tend to lose their looks.
I can't deny that, as the boob and I are getting older,
I think I find I'm more inclined to be a firm book-holder.

You can hold a book for half an hour in bed before you sleep
but try it with a boob – you're lucky if you get a peep.
You can grasp a book in one hand while the other holds the candle
but, as you know, a boob in bed requires both hands to handle.

While you're still young and virile, chasing boobs is fair enough
but once you're over seventy the going gets quite rough.
Books, staying on their shelves, are not impossible to follow
but boobs, forever moving, on the whole are hard to swallow.

Boobs wither, sag and wrinkle, which with age is not so strange.
Books may grow old and yet their shapes and contents rarely change.

In Praise of Ample Femininity

Though sometimes I was criticised and often I've been blamed
because my writing praised the fuller figure,
I can't see, for the life of me, why I should be ashamed
of my belief that beautiful is bigger.

I never once extolled a skinny bird or tiny tits
but ever eulogised well-rounded form,
preferring more to concentrate on well-developed bits
which I consider firmly as the norm.

All women cannot be the same, as I have come to know.
A lot depends on climate, race and breeding
and I would be the last to fault whatever they may show
when much depends on exercise and feeding.

But, when she's well-endowed, possessing reasonable girth,
a buxom beauty's Nature's greatest gift to Man on Earth.

Maori Women

I knew three Maori women once
quite unlike any other.
Two charming Maori maidens and
their quite fantastic mother.

The daughters both were beautiful
as anyone could see
but the mother, proud and dutiful,
was fairest of those three.

She was a pirinitete
a princess of her race
with figure of a Goddess and
a haughty, noble face.

With either of those daughters I,
their favours might have earned
but, to secure the mother's love,
I constantly was spurned.

So I gave up my vain pursuit
although I sorely missed her
for I, who failed to win her love,
succeeded with each sister.

Rangi and Papa

Nothingness was the beginning;
out of Nothing came the Night.
From the Night came Father Rangi,
from the Night came Mother Papa;
Rangi-Papa joined together
joined together and, in coupling,
thus created first the land.
When the world was just beginning,
when there were no stars or planets,
when there was no sun or moon,
long before all living creatures,
long before the time of Man,
then the world was all in darkness;
absolute and utter darkness
not a ray of light.
Rangi was the Great Sky Father;
Papa was the Great Earth Mother.
God and goddess born eternal,
clinging fast to one another
close together, warm, embracing
like a pair of ardent lovers;
arms entwined around each other
indivisible together.

Mating, bore they six male children
gods in human shape they bore
and those children lived between them,
in their closeness lay between them,
little space and little comfort
where the children lay confined:
Tane god of birds and forests,
Tu, the god of war and hunting,
Rongo god of crops and planting,
Haumia, god of all wild foods,

Tawhiri the god of weather,
thunder, lightning, winds and storms;
Tangaroa, god of oceans
and all creatures of the seas.
These, of all Te Papa's children
were the most important gods.

Nestled mid the breasts of Papa
underneath the weight of Rangi,
hot and cramped it was and clammy
dark and airless, hot and sweaty,
till one morning, Papa stirring,
let the fresh air flow between
let light through beneath her armpit
and the gods had space to move;
breathed the fresh cool air of space
saw the light that lit the darkness.
Then the gods discussed between them
how to keep apart their parents
so they might have space forever,
so they always would have light
and enjoy fresh air to breathe.

First suggested Tu, the fiercest,
he, the god of war and violence::
"Let us Rangi kill and Papa
so they cannot lie together,
so they can be pulled apart."
Next up spake Tane-mahuta
disagreeing with his brother:
"It is better not to kill them
but to move them far apart,
leaving thus a space between them
letting in fresh air and light,
letting Rangi be as stranger
in the sky above the earth,
letting Papa stay below him
nurturing all living creatures."

All agreed with Tane's counsel
all except the dark Tawhiri,
he, the god of winds and weather,
feared his kingdom would be threatened
if the light and space intruded.

One by one the gods attempted;
first was Rongo, straining hard;
Tangaroa followed next
joined by Haumia, his sibling,
even their combined strength foundered,
all their efforts met with failure,
even Tu with all his vigour
failed to raise the stubborn Rangi.
Rangi and their mother Papa
still remained secure together.
Forth stepped Tane, flexed his muscles,
but, instead of standing upright,
lay down with his back on Papa,
firmly pressed his feet on Rangi,
with his strong legs pushing upward,
straining very bulging sinew
till, with cries of pain and parting,
sky and earth were prised apart.
Rangi's arms were torn and bleeding
making red the sky at evening
and the red sky of the dawning.

Thus the earth and sky were parted;
thus all Rangi-Papa's children
gained the light and space to move,
breathed the air that flows between;
grew in strength with healthy bodies,
flourished strong and multiplied.
Tane threw the stars to heaven,
also threw the moon and sun
that his father might be dressed
Rangi now looked very handsome.

But the tears of Rangi, falling,
often drench the breasts of Papa
often too the grieving Papa
shakes and trembles in her sorrow.
When the mists rise from the forests,
from the warmth of Papa's body,
Papatuanuku is sighing,
sighing for the arms of Rangi.

Warring of the Gods

You have heard how Ranginui
and his Papatuanuku
by the god Tane-mahuta
were so cruelly torn apart;
how their children for the first time:
Tane, god of birds and forests,
Tu, the god of war and hunting,
Rongo, god of crops and planting,
Haumia, god of all wild foods,
Tawhiri, the god of weather,
thunder, lightning, winds and storms;
Tangaroa, god of oceans
and all creatures of the seas,
had some space to move in freedom,
saw the light and breathed fresh air.
While the others by agreement
acquiesced the separation,
Tawhiri was very angry,
he, the god of storm and tempest,
thunder, lightning, wind and weather.
Angered at his parents parting,
angered by their separation;
could not bear to hear their crying
or to feel the tears of Rangi;
vowed to take revenge or utu
swore to wreak his retribution.
So he rose to join with Rangi
where he fostered many offspring:
winds of North, South, East and West,
clouds of many kinds and colours,
squalls and whirlwinds, fierce tornadoes,
hurricanes and thunderstorms.
So the great Tawhirimatea
gathered armies of his offspring;

from each quarter of the compass
launched them to attack his brothers.

As the winds and gales attack them
Tane's mighty trees are shattered,
snapped and smashed or felled uprooted,
Tane's forests devastated.
Then Tawhiri smites the oceans,
sending storms to strike the seas.
Monumental waves he rouses,
giant waterspouts and whirlpools,
devastating, vast tsunamis
flood the shores of Mother Papa.
Tangaroa flees in panic,
fish seek shelter in deep waters
reptiles seek the flattened forests.
Next Tawhiri seeks his brothers,
hunts for Rongo and Haumia,
gods of food and sustenance.
Mother Papa is determined
for the sake of all her children
that the foods should be protected.
Underground she hides them safely
so Tawhiri cannot find them.
Turning on Tumatauenga,
Tawhiri attacks the war god;
lightning bolts he hurls at Tu.
Tumatau alone withstands him,
Tu alone stands fast against him,
and, against his strength and courage,
Tawhiri cannot prevail.

Then Tawhiri's rage subsided;
calm and peace were reinstated,
Tane's forests, wrecked and ruined,
gradually rejuvenated;

Papa's swamped and flooded shorelines
gradually became restored.
But the anger of the brothers
and their spite against each other
once aroused was not abated.
Tangaroa resented Tane
giving refuge to his reptiles,
giving spears, canoes and fishhooks
from his wood to Tu's descendants,
fishermen with spears and fishhooks,
so he swamps canoes and drowns them,
sweeps away and swamps the shoreline,
washing land and trees and houses
out to sea in flood and fury.

Meditating Tane's actions,
how he forced the separation
of his parents from each other,
he, Tumatauenga pondered.
From the flax plant rauhia
from the flaxen fibre, muka,
fashioned Tu, the god of hunting,
snares to catch the birds of Tane;
from the forest vines and creepers,
and the sturdy flaxen fibre
fashioned nets to catch the fishes
of the sea-god Tangaroa.
From the branches of the forest,
Tu made hoes to dig from Papa
Rongo and Haumia in hiding.
So the birds are caught for cooking;
Fish are heaped along the shoreline;
By their hair, from loosened Papa,
Tu pulls up the food from hiding
grown by Rongo and Haumia.
Tu becomes the god of mankind,

Tu-the-man now eats his brothers
to repay them for their cowardice.
Only Tawhiri, the dauntless,
Tu cannot subdue or conquer.
So the hurricanes and tempests,
cruel revenge of fierce Tawhiri,
Tawhirimatea's utu
ravage still the human race.

Uenuku and the Mist

In the days of ancient legend,
in the early Age of Man,
lived on earth a manly atua,
Uenuku of the Rainbow,
he, "The-Great-Bow-in-the-Sky".
While, before the light of morning,
wandering in the shadowed forest,
came he to a tiny lakeshore.
In the lake, two women bathing
in the cool and crystal waters,
caught the atua's attention
and he stopped to watch them bathing.
From the sky had they descended;
one, Hinepukohurangi,
also known as Tairiakohu,
she, the "Woman-of-the-Mist".
Her companion was her sister
Hinewai, the gentle shower,
she, the "Lady-of-Light-Rain."
To the first spoke Uenuku,
asked he whither she had happened
and the woman answered softly
"We are come from Rangiroa,
from the Rangimaomao.
We are creatures of the darkness
and the cloudy skies of Heaven."
Hinewai then called her sister,
"Come, Hinepukohurangi!
See the sunlight now appears,
it is time for us to go."
Tairiakohu was attracted
to the handsome Uenuku
but the daylight was approaching,
in the eastern sky appearing

with her sister rose, she ascending
forthwith to the skies and heavens.

In the night that follows daytime
Uenuku sat alone
in his whare by the fireside
musing pensively and dreaming,
thinking only of the woman,
she, the "Woman-of-the-Mist".
As the fire and flames subsided,
dying down and dully glowing,
Uenuku heard soft voices
murmuring outside his door.
Then the door was gently opened
and Hinepukohurangi
stood there, waiting to be taken,
waiting for his arms and welcome.
So they spent the night together
spent the night in love together
but, at first-light of the morning,
she rejoined her younger sister
and departed for their home.
Every night came Tairiakohu
to the house of Uenuku
but she warned him that her visits
must be kept a sacred secret.
Warned him not to tell his people
of her secret nightly visits.
"But I long to show your beauty
to my tribe" said Uenuku.
"Time will come, if you are patient,
when we bear a child between us.
Then you may inform your tribesmen,
I will claim you as my husband
but, until that time, our union
must remain between us secret
only shared with Hinewai.

Should you e'er divulge our secret,
then shall I be forced to leave you.

Fearful of his lover leaving,
Uenuku kept the secret
but as with the passing months
pride in his celestial wife
grew within his breast to bursting.
He could not resist the telling
or to boast about her beauty.
Quickly news spread through the village;
there were some who longed to see her,
others simply disbelieved him
urging him to let them see her.
"No, I cannot," he protested,
"for each morning, prior to daylight,
with her sister she departs."
Village elders then advised him:
"You must block up every opening,
block up every crack and crevice
and, in first light of the morning,
thus pretending it is dark,
she, deceived and with you staying,
when the morning light appears,
we can pull the door and see her,
prove the truth of what you tell us."

Uenuku to this counsel
with reluctance now agreed;
spent the daytime blocking openings,
every tiny crack and crevice.
In the darkness of the night-time
lay with arms around his wife.
In the very early morning
came the voice of Hinewai.
"I can hear my sister calling.
It is time for me to go."

Thus Hinepukohurangi
softly spoke to Uenuku.
"No!" He said, "You are mistaken.
See the whare is in darkness!"
Thus he answered Tairiakohu
but the voice of Hinewai
called more loudly and, in anguish,
springing from her husband's side
opening the whare door,
now she stood revealed in sunlight;
long black hair her only cover
as the watching men and women
gazed at her in admiration.
Long the moment that she stood there
then with loud despairing cry,
shrinking back into the whare,
back into the gloom and darkness,
hid beneath the darkened shadows.

Uenuku came out proudly,
sat upon the outer threshold.
Hine, hiding in the darkness,
sang to him with tears and sadness,
"Uenuku, my beloved!
You have now betrayed my trusting;
shown me when the star of morning
and the eastern sun has risen,
so the cries of Hinewai,
so the warnings of my sister
as we lay within your whare,
reached me not and I am shamed
in the sight of all your people."
Rising she approached the doorway,
naked stood before the whare,
rose up swiftly to the gable.
Uenuku tried to grasp her
but her mist slipped through his fingers
swirled around and rose above him.

Like two clouds the two flew upwards
as Hinepukohurangi
and her sister Hinewai
rose into the distant heavens,
finally were lost to sight.
Never were they seen again.

Uenuku was remorseful
realised what he had done
left his village and his people
travelled through the wide world searching
in the valleys and the gullies
in the forests and the woodlands
in the bush and barren plateaux,
mountain tops and sandy beaches
searching for his lost beloved
till his hair turned grey and thinner
and he had grown old and withered.
Then the great Sky Father, Rangi,
pitied him and all his suffering,
lifted him into the heavens
changed him to a shining rainbow.
When you see, in early morning,
white mist rising from the bushland
and you see a shining rainbow
arching high across the heavens,
then you know that Uenuku
and Hinepukoherangi
reconciled with wrongs forgiven
are together once again.

Mataora and Niwareka

In the land called Rarohenga
lived the fair-skinned Turehu;
women of the underworld,
underworld of Te Reinga.
Beautiful with flowing tresses
like white plumes of toetoe,
white hair falling to the waistline.
Nothing wore they but an apron
made of rimurimu seaweed.
Often, in the early morning
when the mortals still were sleeping
Turehu would go to visit
upper Te Ao Turoa
Upper World of men and mortals.
To Te Raraoterangi,
house of chieftain Mataora,
came a party of Turehu
led by princess Niwareka.
Mataora was awakened
by the chatter of the women,
rose and cooked some food for breakfast
offered cooked food to his guests
but the women would not eat it
tasted it but would not eat it.

Mataora at his fishpond
caught a basketful of herrings
offering the uncooked herrings,
raw to the Turehu women..
Ravenously they were eaten.
Then, to thank him for the fishes,
all the women danced a haka,
lifting high their feet and stamping
arms and hands gesticulating,
weaving in and out and under.

Niwareka to the forefront,
gracefully she led the dancers,
singing: "Here is Niwareka."
and the women called in answer:
"Niwareka, Niwareka."
Oh! The chief was so enchanted;
never had he seen such dancing,
never limbs so lithe and graceful,
and the chieftain Mataora
fell in love with Niwareka,
loved her for her gracious bearing,
her demeanour and decorum
and the beauty of her body.
She, returning his affection,
when her friends had all departed,
Niwareka stayed behind;
stayed to live with Mataora
and that night became his wife.

Happily they lived together
till the chieftain's elder brother,
Tautoro, became enamoured
of his brother's lovely bride.
Niwareka always faithful,
never once betrayed her husband.
Though she spurned his faithless brother,
Mataora was hot-tempered,
grew suspicious of Tautoro,
lost his trust in Niwareka
and, inflamed with jealous rage,
shouting baseless accusations,
struck her with his open hand
beat her with his fist and thrashed her.
Niwareka was astounded,
gravely hurt and sore dismayed.

Never back in Rarohenga
had she suffered such experience.
Cruelty, abuse and anger,
were unknown in Rarohenga.

Bruised and bleeding, shocked and weeping,.
Forthwith fled she to her homeland.
Desolate without her presence,
Mataora then pursued her
though the path was long he followed.
came he to Kuwatawata,
he, the guardian of the doorways;
from him learned that Niwareka
had already passed by, weeping.
So, the old Kuwatawata
for the pleading Mataora,
drew the bolts and threw wide open,
opened wide the doorway leading
to the underworld below.
Mataora started downwards,
there he met with Tiwaiwaka
she, the flitting, chattering fantail,
undertook to be his guide.

To the house of Uetonga,
father royal of Niwareka,
Tiwaiwaka led his footsteps.
Uetonga bade him welcome,
busy though he was tattooing.
Mataora watched in wonder
as the old man with a chisel
on a warrior's face and forehead
cut deep grooves and made the blood flow
as he made a tattoo, moko.
Mataora cried in horror:
"That is not the way to tattoo!
See my moko, how it's painted,
painted on in flowing patterns,
flowing lines which cause no pain."

Uetonga placed two fingers
on the face of Mataora,
smeared the chieftain's painted moko.
"That is fit for painted patterns
on the rafters of a whare.
See this mat with patterned border,
Taniko by women fashioned?
That is like your painted moko.
See this mere carved of kauri,
as we carve the kauri deeply,
so we carve the face and buttocks
that man's beauty may not vanish
thus we make a man's true moko."
When the young men saw besmeared
Mataora's painted moko,
loud they laughed and loudly mocked him,
disrespectfully derided.

Mataora begged Uetonga
pleaded for a proper moko
in the fashion of turehu.
Uetonga then consented.
On the morrow Mataora
prone upon the ground submitted
to the torture of the chisel.
Waves of pain flowed and engulfed him
and to give his soul endurance
in his agony and weakness
Mataora sang this song:

"Niwareka! Say, where are you?
"Show yourself, my Niwareka!
"See my love for you has brought me
"to your homeland, Niwareka.
"Love devours me Niwareka!
"Come to me, my Niwareka!
"Niwareka! Niwareka!
"To the upper world come with me

"Leave your homeland, Niwareka
"End my long-enduring pain!"

Niwareka's younger sister,
Uekura, while in passing,
heard the song of Mataora
heard the oft-repeated naming
of her sister Niwareka
and she ran to tell her sister
to a place called Taranaki
where she found her sister weaving,
in the house of Uetonga;
weaving Te Raupapanui,
chieftain's garment for her father;
told her story to her sister
of the unknown stranger chanting,
Niwareka's name repeating
often in his karakia
while their father made his moko.
Niwareka laid to one side
Uetonga's cloak-in-making
spread mats on the ground around it
under a pohutukawa.
Uekura she commanded:
"When the tattooing is finished,
bring this young man when recovered,
bring him to this tree"

When the stranger had recovered
Uekura led him thither.
He was tall and strong and handsome
with his finely crafted moko.
While admiring girls surrounded.
Niwareka watched him closely
though appearance changed by moko,
knew the garments he was wearing,
garments she herself had woven,
recognized the crafted patterns,

knew that he was Mataora,
recognized him as her husband
and to him was reconciled.

Mataora was uneasy
in the Underworld embarrassed
when his brother Te Whirirau
killed in battle years before
now invited Mataora
to his home in Rangaahua
and his brother-in-law Tauwehe
who had died ten years before
pressed him with an invitation
that he should with Niwareka
stay with him in Raronenga.
Mataora now entreated
Niwareka to return
with him to Te Ao Turoa.
But he found his wish to leave them
met with much strong opposition
from her relatives and family.
Uetonga put it plainly:
"You may go but leave my daughter,
where she need not live in fear.
Here, no fear of being beaten,
needs her happiness to cloud."
Tauwehe added bluntly:
"Upper World is dark with evil,
violence and evil temper.
Here is only light and goodness
spirits who have shared our goodness
never wish to earth return."
Mataora was ashamed
thus to hear the world so blamed
but desire and his resolve
to return remained unshaken.
Then he made a solemn promise
to observe the peaceful customs

back in Te Ao Turoa
that he'd learned in Rarohenga.
So, the father Uetonga
gave the couple then his blessing,
gave his blessing to their journey
back into the Upper World.
Gave a cloak to Mataora,
gave Te Rangihaupapa
and the belt wherewith to fasten
Te Rurukuoterangi.
So the couple headed upwards
from the realm of Rarohenga
till they reached Kuwatawata,
he, the guardian of the doorways
to the Underworld below
and the Upper World above.
And Kuwatawata asked him:
"Do you take, from Rarohenga,
any souvenirs of value?"
Mataora showed his Moko
Niwareka showed him nothing
but the guardian asked the princess:
"Show me what is in your bundle?"
Fearing loss by confiscation
of the cloak Rangihaupapa
and Rurukuoterangi,
Niwareka answered falsely
"It is just a few old garments".
but the guardian, grabbed the bundle,
seized the cloak and held it firmly,
angrily pronounced an edict
that, from this time forth, no mortal
from the realm of Rarohenga
may to Ao Turoa return:
"To Te Po and to Te Ao!
men henceforth will pass but one way
on this road of no return!"

Finally, Kuwatawata
gave the cloak to Niwareka
sent them upward on their journey.
At Te Raraoterangi
where their friends soon gathered round them,
all the women showing interest
in the garments and the patterns
Niwareka brought to show them
but the men were fascinated,
envied Mataora's moko.
Thus the husband and his wife
brought back gifts from Rarohenga
he, the skilful art of tattoo
she the patterns used in weaving
and the garments of Turehu.

But the most important lesson
which they brought Te Ao Turoa
was the message of Uetonga:
strength to counter and control
evil rage and fiery temper
is of greater consequence
than the patterns or the moko.
Never more did Mataora
beat or shout at Niwareka

Rona in the Moon

By the lake called Te Waiora
lived a woman of great beauty
in their whare by the lakeside
with her husband and two children
dearly loved and quite contented
Rona seemed the perfect wife
but their peace was sometimes spoiled
by her quick and fiery temper
and the sharpness of her tongue.
Came the day her husband said:
"I will take the children fishing
for tonight the full moon favours
fishing near the offshore island
where the fish are plentiful.
We will go and catch some fish there.
We will not return tonight
but tomorrow night expect us
when out nets are full of fishes
with a goodly catch returning
hoping you will have a meal
cooked and ready for us waiting.
We will all be tired and hungry."

So he sailed off with the children
leaving Rona all alone
in the whare by the lakeside.
On the next day Rona gathered
twigs and firewood for the umu,
carefully prepared the oven,
set the wood around the stones
placed the twigs between the boulders,
set the hangi oven right.
covered it with leaves and branches
wrapped the food in puki leaves
placed it ready in the umu.

When the evening shadows lengthened
Rona lit the cooking fire,
took a calabash for water
from the nearby gushing spring.
Needing water for the hangi
when the stones were red and glowing,
when the boulders in the hangi
heated by the burning wood
gave off steam when doused with water
then that steam would cook the food.

As she lit the twigs and firewood
she could hear the sound of singing
songs of the returning fishers.
Quickly covered up the umu
with a layer of fresh earth
tramped it carefully to firm it
so the oven was made ready.
Now she hurried down the pathway,
hurried with her calabash
to the spring of gushing water
water which would douse the hangi.
Darkness fell before she reached it
for the path was long and winding
but the silver moon was shining
and it lit the winding pathway
so she saw the track quite clearly.
Suddenly the moon was hidden
by a passing cloud obscured.
Rona could not see the pathway
stubbed her toe against a tree root
fell against a rock in darkness
grazed her shin and cried in pain.
In her pained exasperation
Rona cursed the moon in anger

Cursed the moon for light withholding
shouted out "Pokokohua"
meaning "cooked head" as an insult.

Then the moon was very angry,
hearing that malignant curse
angry at that shouted insult.
She descended from the heavens
seized rude Rona by her hair
lifted Rona from her footing
bearing her towards the heavens.
Rona seized a branch of Ngaio,
clung to it with all her might
desperately gripped the ngaio
but the goddess was the stronger
and the ngaio tree pulled loose
from the earth, from Mother Papa,
all its roots were torn apart.
Rona then was borne far skywards
upwards to our Father, Rangi,
carrying her calabash
holding firmly to the ngaio
carried far into the heaven
far into the starlit night-sky
carried by the angry moon
placed upon the silver moon face
where she can be seen whenever
full-bodied the moon is shining.

Oh! It was a sad homecoming
for the father and the children!
Not a sign of mother Rona
not a trace of her they found.
When they opened up the umu
all the food was burned and toasted
none of it was cooked or steamed.
Then they looked into the night sky
saw upon the moon's full face

Rona, wife and mother held there
holding still her calabash
holding still the ngaio tree
and they realised that Rona
with her hot and fiery temper
and the sharpness of her tongue
somehow tempted gods too far.

Sometimes, when the night is still
you can hear a woman crying
calling to her man and children.
Some say it's Ruru the morepork
others, Matuku the bittern,
or the crying of karoro
or the sounding whale, tohora,
but I think that it is Rona
calling for her man and children.

Pania of the Reef

In the wide Pacific Ocean,
E Moana-nui-a-kiwa,
to the south of many islands
lies the land Aotearoa,
named by Pakeha: 'New Zealand'.
On the east coast of North Island
known as Ta-Ika-a-Maui,
East Coast tahatika whiti
near the cliffs of Hukarere,
where the river Ahuriri
meets the blue Pacific waters,
lived a lovely ocean maiden.
Very beautiful was Pania,
not a dreaded ponaturi
but with human form and figure.
Loveliest of all the sea-sprites
as she swam among the fishes
with the creatures of her reef world,
with the other ocean maidens
in the sunlight of the daytime,
in the happy, sparkling waters,
as they splashed with songs and dances
light and lithesome as the sea-spray
leaping, dancing on the waters.

In the evenings, after sunset
when the sunlight had departed
and the shadows of the evening
crept across the ocean waters,
when the breezes chilled their bodies
all the other ocean maidens
dived into the depths below.
Only Pania swam alone.
to the river Ahuriri.
There, along a special stream

where the sweetest water flowed
from a spring enclosed by mosses,
she would lie amongst the raupo,
while the moon rose in the heavens
and the silver stars appeared,
rest among the tall flax bushes
each night hidden in their shelter
but returning to the ocean
at the first grey light of dawning.

Karitoki was a chief's son,
handsome, young and full of vigour.
Every evening after sunset,
when the moon was in the heavens
and the stars were shining silver
he would come to quench his thirst
at the spring amongst the mosses
where the sweetest water flowed.
Unaware of Pania's presence,
never knowing she observed him
as he shed his cloak, kaitaka,
shed his skirt and, without clothing,
bathed himself in flowing water.
Thus it was for many evenings
till one night as she observed him,
Pania whispered a faint sigh
and it carried on the breeze
to the ears of Karitoki.
Turning round, he was astonished
to discover in the moonlight
Pania laid amongst the reeds,
hiding in the flax and raupo.

Never had he seen such beauty
or such absolute perfection
as the loveliness of Pania
now emerging from her hiding.
In her eyes he saw the love-light;
straightway then his heart was smitten;
forthwith fell in love with Pania
and he took her to his whare
where, in secret, in the darkness,
they became as man and wife.
But at first grey light of dawning
Pania rose, prepared to leave him.
Karitoki tried to stop her
so she carefully explained
that, unless she reached the ocean
when she heard the sirens calling,
joined her sisters in the daylight,
her survival would be threatened,
she would wither, pine and die
but she promised every evening
to return to Karitoki.
So their marriage was continued,
every evening to his whare
Pania faithfully returned
but at first light every morning
she would swim back to the ocean
to rejoin the ocean maidens.

In the daytime, to companions,
Karitoki often boasted,
boasted of the perfect beauty
of the absolute perfection
of his ocean maiden wife.
But his friends did not believe him
for no one had ever seen her
for she only came in darkness
and was gone before each dawn.
Karitoki was frustrated

that nobody would believe him,
that they mocked him and derided,
called him whakapehapeha,
called him boaster, fool and braggart.
He consulted with an elder,
a most learned kaumatua,
as to how he might restrain her,
stop her leaving him each dawning.
And the wise man said: "That's easy!
If cooked food she ever swallows
she will not then be permitted
to rejoin her ocean sisters."
So that night, while she was sleeping,
Karitoki placed a morsel
of cooked food in Pania's mouth.
But Ruru the morepork loudly
from the treetops called a warning,
waking Pania from her love-sleep.
Startled, Pania on awaking
spat the morsel from her mouth.
Horrified that Karitoki
should thus place her life in danger,
jeopardising her survival,
Pania fled straight from his whare
ran and dived into the water,
swam until she reached the ocean
where her sisters gladly surfaced
and, with loving arms around her,
drew her down into the depths.
Karitoki, frantically
swam in vain about the ocean,
searched in vain for his beloved
who he never saw again.

But some folk of Hukarere,
by the mouth of Ahuriri,
looking deep into the water
by the reef where Pania dwelt,

swear that they can see her lying
in the depths below the surface
with her arms outstretched, appealing.

Who can say if she's imploring
explanation for his falsehood
or expressing her undying
love for faithless Karitoki...?

The Phantom Canoe

On the lake Rotomahana,
near the mountain Tarawera,
Guide, Sophia Hinerangi,
piloted a group of tourists,
Pakeha who were returning
from a trip to Te Tarata
and Otukapuarangi.
Famous were those White and Pink
terraces of Tuhourangi,
called the world's eighth natural wonder.
In a whaleboat now returning
to the Te Ariki landing
near the village of Moura
thence to dine at Te Wairoa
seven others made the journey,
one, a Clergyman among them,
Justice of the Peace another,
all mature and worthy people.

Suddenly, before their vision,
from the evening mist appearing,
less than half a mile in distance,
all perceived an apparition,
ten men in a war canoe
kairakau a group of warriors
each with hair dressed as for burial
plumed with feathers of the huia
white makura of kotuku.
Silently those warriors paddled,
deft their strokes and skilled their rhythm
yet the waka stayed unmoving,
not a ripple broke the surface
as the evening sunlight glistened
on the smooth and crystal waters.

Swiftly as their sudden coming,
rapidly they disappeared,
vanished in the misty silence;
neither sign nor shade remaining,
just the calm, unbroken surface
of the lake Rotomahana.

Back at last in Te Wairoa,
guide Sophia told the story,
to the old and wise Tohunga,
Te Tuhoto, old and wizened,
told him of the eerie vision
which the others also witnessed.
Gravely spoke the old Tohunga:
"Often have I warned the people
that the gods would wreak their vengeance,
punish their depraved behaviour.
What you saw upon the water
was no earthly waka-taua
but a signal from the spirits
of ancestors, waka-wairua,
to foretell a great disaster
which will overtake our village."

Ten days later, after midnight,
(June 10th 1886),
suddenly the earth was shaken;
violent and recurrent earthquakes,
followed by a loud explosion
as the mountain peaks erupted,
blasting fiery columns upward,
hurling molten rock and ashes
several thousand metres high.
Black clouds formed above the columns
lit by angry, lurid lightning;
thunderous was the mountain's roaring.
At 3.30 in the morning
Roto's bed blew out completely

and a rain of mud and ashes,
boiling mud and burning ashes,
fell upon the earth surrounding.

Buried were the lakeside people
Te Ariki and Moura -
of the six score Maori hunga,
none escaped those lethal showers.
Te Wairoa was also buried;
tragic was the loss of life.
Tarawera changed completely;
none could recognise the lake;
all the land was devastated,
Tikitapu bush was flattened
and the Pink and White world wonders,
pink Otukapuarangi
and the whiter Te Tarata
disappeared beneath the debris,
utterly destroyed forever.

Still today at Te Wairoa
you can see the buried village,
see the old Tohunga's whare
and the hut of guide Sophia;
see the remnants of the smithy,
bakery, hotel and flour mill
excavated from the debris,
from the cloak of mud and ashes;
see the line of trees now growing,
growing from the buried fence-posts
testament to that disaster -
but of pink or white terraces
widely known as eighth world-wonder,
not a trace remains...

The Lost Pink and White Terraces of Rotomahana

Many famed and wealthy tourists used to come from far and wide
to visit Rotorua, whence they'd take a coach or ride
for Te Wairoa village, there to hire a stout canoe
to transport them across the lake, the Terraces to view.

Otukapuarangi was the favoured one with wide
pink basins of blue water where a man could warm his hide.
Te Tarata, also beautiful, like marble glistening white,
was quite nearby and judged to be a truly awesome sight.

The pair, by some, were then considered as the world's eighth wonder
but, when the Mount erupted, were completely buried under
a cloak of mud and lava which set solid like cement.
Today, no single trace remains to prove the argument.

Now, the iwi of Moura by the lake Rotomahana
and kainga Te Ariki, had considerable mana
as guides and one-night hosts (for which they charged the tourists fees)
and, with their new-found wealth, were living lives of slothful ease.

The fire-god, Tarawera, dwelling in the Mountain's cavity,
was angered when he saw his peoples' indolent depravity.
When rash youths ate his sacred honey, he became annoyed
and so, those wicked peoples' lives and living he destroyed.

The story of his vengeance I have written down for you
in a poem posted yesterday entitled "The Phantom Canoe"
but I hope Charles Blomfield's painting of the Terrace, well contrived,
will give you an impression of that which we are deprived.

The Mission Church at Te Mu

Inspired by missionary zeal and Samuel Marsden's piety,
the Reverend Seymour Spencer with his family and wife,
after two years with the London Mission Church Society,
decided that New Zealand was the place to spend his life.

In 1844 he moved from Taupo to Kariri
and worked among the Maoris there till after '52
when, being of new evangelistic challenge never weary,
he relocated to the abandoned mission at Te Mu.

His effort was impeded by the 1860 war
and the later popularity of nearby Te Wairoa
with European tourists who invaded, by the score,
the sinter terraces that graced Rotomahana's shore.

The photo at the left shows Spencer's small church at Te Mu
where he re-established and set up his little mission station.
There, with his wife, through unrelenting zeal, attendance grew
among his Maori converts to substantial congregation.

On the right we see the ruin, left in 1886,
of all that he had striven to achieve, through faith and prayers,
when erupting Tarawera played its devastating tricks
and Te Wairoa, quite buried, was abandoned left, for years.

It's often said: "The Lord gives but He also takes away"
and Maoris claimed the cataclysm born of godly wrath.
The pathetic ruin, mud-covered, stands as evidence today
that He did not exempt the work done by this man-of-cloth.

In 1870, Seymour, with his family, retired
to Maketu – all hopes buried now to which he had aspired.

dedicated with love to my friend Maureen Bleiler

The Legend of Hinemoa and Tutanekai

In the village of Owhata
by the sparkling eastern waters
of the deep Lake Rotorua,
lived a lovely Maori maiden,
beautiful in every feature.
None surpassed her gracious nature
or accomplishment and learning;
none could match her lithesome figure,
none could boast a higher ranking
than the princess Hinemoa.
Umukaria. her father,
chief of all the Ngati Arawa
had declared his daughter puhi
had proclaimed her tapu (sacred).
When she reached the age of marriage
then her husband would be chosen
by the elders of her hapu,
by the iwi (tribal) elders
and the members of her family.
At the frequent council meetings
where the chiefs all met together,
those beholding Hinemoa
were immediately smitten.
All who saw her loved her madly,
sought to gain her hand in marriage
but her tribe their suits rejected
for their mana was too lowly
and their ranking too inferior.
Suitors came from far and wide
offering whakapati bribe,
seeking Hine's hand as bride
but rejected by her tribe.

On the island of Mokoia
in the centre of the roto,
lived a family of brothers;
brave Tutanekai the youngest,
born of an illicit union
when his mother took a lover
but her husband then forgave her,
spared their lives and sought no utu,
raised the baby as his son.
All the young man's elder brothers
love for Hinemoa declared
but, the same as all the others,
none had any better fared.

Best at games Tutanekai was,
he could hurl the huata farthest,
he could whirl the tiaha fastest,
he could strike with mere hardest.
None could run as fast as he ran,
none could leap as high as he leapt
or jump over wider rivers.
None could better him at wrestling,
none could match his strength and muscle,
none had such coordination,
or excelled in skills of battle
and, on seeing Hinemoa,
with her beauty he was smitten,
fell in love with her, despairing
of his lowly situation.
Lowest born of all his brothers,
born without a legal father,
knowing well that Hine's family

and the elders of her hapu
as a suitor would reject him.

But Tutanekai was handsome
and one day when Hinemoa,
working with the women, weaving
rauhuia for fine kaitaka,
flaxen cloak for chief, her father,
trimmed with roa kiwi feathers,
saw Tutanekai appraising
as he watched her nimble fingers,
saw the love-light in his gazing,
saw the longing in his looking.
Then her heart began to falter
and her sight with tears was misted
and her hands began to tremble
and her legs and knees were shaking
and she felt that she was fainting
for with love her heart was vanquished.

At each later council meeting,
seeing each the other distant,
daring no communication,
not a word or sign permitted,
only furtive, longing glances
as their mutual love developed.
Opportunity none given
for their love to be requited
and Tutanekai sat sadly
in the growing dusk of twilight
on the shoreline of Mokoia
till the waters ceased to sparkle
and he played disconsolately
on his flute, so melancholy
and the sound of his lamenting
in the stillness of the evening

wafted, sad, across the waters
to the heart of Hinemoa
where she sat with passion aching
and she vowed to marry no-one
but Tutanekai her true love.

Every night she heard his music
while the weeks and months passed slowly
and the people then suspected,
as all suitors she rejected,
that she had a secret lover
somewhere far across the water.
To prevent clandestine meeting,
Umukaria her father,
ordered all canoes and paddles
all the waka and the hoea
to be dragged above the shoreline
out of reach of lapping waters,
out of reach of Hinemoa.
But night after night she listened
to the sad flute music calling
and her heart was filled with longing;
she could bear the pain no longer.
So, one night, in depth of darkness
when the village fast was sleeping,
te kainga tuumoe,
stealing six gourds from the kitchen,
creeping softly to the lakeside,
to moana Rotorua,
the despairing Hinemoa
slipped into the silent waters.

Firmly tied the calabashes
to her arms to keep her buoyant
and she struck out for Mokoia
with the strains of flute to guide her.

Many hours she swam on bravely
till she reached Mokoia safely
but the coldness of the water
chilled her bones and numbed her body
so she headed for the hot pool
where she saw the steam arising
Waikimihia they call it.
As the hot pool warmed her body,
and her spirits were recovered
she was conscious of her bareness,
far too shy to enter naked
in the house of her beloved.

Now, Tutanekai was thirsty
and he laid his flute beside him,
sent his servant for some water
with a calabash he sent him
to the stream of cool, clear water
near the pool where Hinemoa
had concealed her naked body.
As the servant was returning
with the calabash of water,
Hinemoa called with strange voice,
called to him: "Mo wai te wai?"
and the servant answered softly
"It is for Tutanekai.".
Then demanded Hinemoa:
"Give the calabash to me!"
When the frightened slave obeyed her
Hinemoa took the gourd,
smashed it into little pieces;
dashed the gourd against the poolside.
So the servant hurried homeward;
told Tutanekai what happened
and Tutanekai was puzzled;
sent the servant out again,

sent him on a second errand
giving him another gourd;
told him to return with water.
But the second time it happened
just as had occurred before;
this time also Hinemoa
took and broke the gourd in pieces.
When the unnerved slave reported
now Tutanekai was angry;
armed himself with greenstone mere,
with his club of green pounamu;
went himself down to the hot pool.

At the pool, he loudly challenged,
whosoever might be hiding;
daring him to stand and answer,
calling him to show his face.
Hinemoa gave no answer,
like a mouse, kept still and silent;
not the slightest sound emitted,
hiding her uncovered body
underneath a hanging rock,
trying to afford protection
for her nakedness and shame.
But Tutanekai felt round it,
round the rock where Hine'd hidden,
seized her by her hair and pulled her
upright, so she stood revealed
to his unbelieving vision.
"I am Hinemoa" she told him:
"I have come to be with you."
He could not believe his hearing,
he could not believe his eyes,
never had he seen such beauty
nor such absolute perfection.
Then he put his cloak around her;

took her to his house to sleep
took her to his home, his whare
took her to his bed to keep.

In the morning all the people
as they made their morning meal,
wondered why Tutanekai,
always first to rise from slumber,
slept so late this sunny morning.
And his father grew concerned
thinking that he might be ill
sent a servant to arouse him.

When the slave looked in the whare
saw four feet instead of two
he reported to the father
but the father, disbelieving,
sent the slave to look again.
Now the servant looking closely
saw the sleeping Hinemoa
lying with Tutanekai
so he ran back to the father,
cried aloud in sheer surprise:
"It is Hinemoa who lies
with your son Tutanekai!"
and the brothers, disbelieving,
saw Tutanekai emerging,
Hinemoa on his arm.

Then the people, struck with wonder,
saw canoes approach the island,
knew that Hinemoa's family
coming to collect their daughter
might demand revenge or utu,
and the people feared a war.
Hinemoa would be taken

from Tutanekai forever
and the lovers would be parted.
But when Hinemoa's family
landed and observed the lovers,
saw their daughter safe and happy
saw the lovers' glad demeanour,
then there was a glad rejoicing
and a happy reuniting,
singing, dancing, joyous feasting,
pu korero, many speeches;
and the two tribes came together
in a bond of love and friendship.
Lasting peace was forged between them
through the love of Hinemoa
and the young Tutanekai.

The Whim of Cleopatra

O' haughty queen whose eyes have seen with transport of delight
the deaths obscene of men who've been your lovers overnight.
Their agony you view with glee as poisons course their veins
with stiffening limbs to suit your whims and cruelly clouded brains.

You stuffed up Julius Caesar who had given you the shrug
when you turned up at his hotel room rolled in a Persian rug
but, when he hit the Ides of March and Brutus had him done
the only thing he left you was Caesarion, your son.

So you'd bed those prisoners on the night before their execution
and have them poisoned in the morn to watch their dissolution
but, when there were no prisoners left to share your company,
you decided you would set your sights on Marcus Antony.

Now Antony as a lover boy was not as good as Caesar
for he did not know quite where to go with a woman best to please her
but he brought you silk and asses milk and the finest Roman wine
and told you you looked beautiful so you got along just fine.

Then Julius' successor, one Octavian by name,
thrashed Antony at Actium and spoiled your little game
for, when you heard he'd triumphed and Mark Antony had died,
you had a viper bite your boob, committing suicide.

Thus Nemesis did wait your fate when lost was Egypt's might,
and you went to rest with envenomed breast from the asp's avenging bite.

inspired by the painting "Cleopatra testing poisons on condemned prisoners" by Alexandre Cabanel (Oil on canvas, 1887)

www.ingramcontent.com/pod-product-compliance
Lightning Source LLC
Chambersburg PA
CBHW070726160426
43192CB00009B/1335